D0991353

A SURVEY OF OLD TESTAMENT TEACHING

By
J. WASH WATTS

Volume I
ADAM — DAVID

WINGATE JUNIOR COLLEGE

BROADMAN PRESS
NASHVILLE, TENNESSEE

3480

Copyright, 1947
BROADMAN PRESS
Nashville, Tennessee

Printed in United States of America
1.5-AT49-2

TO
FELLOW STUDENTS OF THE WORD
WHO DESIRE
TO UNDERSTAND THE BIBLE
IN ORDER THAT
THEY MAY PREACH ITS GOSPEL

A SURVEY OF OLD TESTAMENT TEACHING

Jehovah our God is one Jehovah: and thou shalt love Jehovah thy God with all thy heart, and with all thy soul, and with all thy might. And these words, . . . shall be upon thy heart; *and thou shalt teach them diligently.*

—Deuteronomy 6:4-7

Then opened he [Jesus] their mind, that they might understand the scriptures; and he said unto them, . . . *Ye are witnesses of these things.*

—Luke 24:45-48

In any theological treatment, the principles of development are, of course, the conceptions of authors about God. As the Old Testament authors build their teaching concerning God chiefly about the name "Jehovah," the interpretation of "Jehovah" worship must be a paramount issue. From the time when this name first appears on the lips of Eve at the birth of her first-born son, through the great revelations to Moses that make this name a synonym for the moral attributes of God, and in all the teaching of all the prophets, we are led step by step to the conviction that the "Jehovah" of the Old Testament is the Jesus of the New Testament. Accordingly, the fulfilment of all is predicted by the following word of Zechariah as coming in Messiah, "And Jehovah shall be king over all the earth: in that day shall Jehovah be one, and his name one." No amount of care is too dear a price for any student of the Scriptures to pay in order to attain an unclouded view of this truth. We must needs consider this the main objective of all our work.

In all these methods scientific correctness is necessary, but scientific methods need not exclude the phenomena of revelation and faith as credible data. Revelation and faith are naturally not subjects for consideration in a science which deals with physical matter only, but they are vital to a science that is supremely spiritual. In the words of James Orr, "It is Christ Himself in the full revelation of His glory as the only-begotten Son who is the touchstone and measure of the supernatural for faith; and only that view of revelation in Israel is adequate which finds its necessary culmination in His person and redemption.'"[4]

We admit that *our starting viewpoint is one of faith in the trustworthiness of the Bible.* We desire to submit our convictions to objective investigation according to the strictest standards of criticism. Nevertheless, we also believe that it is as scientifically correct for the believer to start from the viewpoint of faith as it is for scientists to start from the viewpoint of any current hypothesis of material science with a view to testing it. Moreover, we believe that the results depend largely upon choice of the right hypothesis. As a surveyor, having found certain old landmarks recorded on a plat of land, runs a line according to them with a view to locating others described by that same plat, so may a believer, who has found in Christ a savior and in many prophetical Scriptures landmarks leading to him, reasonably run a line by faith backward in search of earlier revelations belonging to the same plan indicated by his Bible. The finding of these revelations is likely to depend upon the zeal and judgment with which the believer tests his own convictions about the Bible. The problem is intricate, the issue vital to spiritual development, and the cost fully worth while.

The *class use* of these outlines will include direct Bible study under their guidance, parallel investigation, and class discussion.

---

[4]Orr, James, *The Problem of the Old Testament*, p. 22.

PREFACE

The *purpose* of this study is to guide students of the Bible to those viewpoints from which they may continue Old Testament interpretation independently. It will not undertake to do more than lay foundations. It is prepared primarily for use in the author's classes at the New Orleans Baptist Theological Seminary.

While interpreting the Old Testament we interpret also the New Testament. The harmonious linking of the two is the true objective for such a study. We must needs remember that "Jehovah our God is one Jehovah."[1] The example of Jesus in preparation of the apostles for the preaching of the gospel is likewise significant, for the Scriptures he used when "he opened their minds that they might understand the scriptures"[2] were Old Testament Scriptures. When he said, "Ye are witnesses of these things,"[3] he referred to truths first taught in the Old Testament.

The *methods* of this study will be historical, exegetical, and theological.

The historical background of authors, books, and language will be sought. Lessons from the history of nations whose influence has a bearing on Israelitic history will be introduced, but this must be done largely through citation of parallel reading. It is understood that archeological and critical reviews of such history are closely dovetailed with interpretation, but the mass of such material requires the handling of it by theological seminaries in a separate department of study. Only brief directions for reading will be introduced at points where the information is most pertinent. These will direct atten-

[1]Deut. 6:4. [2]Luke 24:45. [3]Luke 24:48.

vii

tion to outstanding matters and investigation to features of vital concern to our conclusions in interpretation.

Exegetical treatments will include outlines of books and textual notes. Outlines present the teaching in a summary fashion. Notes present explanations concerning details of importance, information not available to all, and emphases upon matters of extraordinary concern to us. Outlines are intended to present the prominent points of the writers of the Scriptures rather than points of chief interest to us, and to do so as far as possible according to a logical arrangement that will enable us to observe the consistent development of their teaching. It does matter a great deal to us and to our preaching of the gospel whether or not we think the Old Testament to be consistent and understandable. Of course no intimation is intended that its men and affairs are always consistent. The question is, Is its message of hope to sinful men, its teaching about "Jehovah," consistent and understandable?

Theological treatment will attempt to lay foundations of Biblical Theology. Whereas Systematic Theology organizes our beliefs according to a system of its own, Biblical Theology does so with reference to their origin in Scripture, thus according to the order of their development in Scripture. Biblical Theology, therefore, maintains a close contact with biblical history and makes the creeds drawn therefrom clear and interesting. It is obviously impossible to give in our work a full treatment of this theology; but, while attention is centered on the history, attempts will be made to lay foundations.

CONTENTS

GENESIS

PAGE

Introduction 1
General Outline 4

Detailed Outlines with Textual Notes:

Gen. 1:1 to 2:3, p. 5; Gen. 2:4 to 4:26, p. 20; Gen. 5:1 to 6:8, p. 47; Gen. 6:9 to 9:29, p. 55; Gen. 10:1 to 11:9, p. 60; Gen. 11:10-26, p. 63; Gen. 11:27 to 26:11, p. 64; Gen. 25:12-18, p. 83; Gen. 25:19 to 35:29, p. 83; Gen. 36:1-43, p. 96; Gen. 37:1 to 50:26, p. 96.

Critical Problems:

I. The Stories of Genesis, p. 13. II. Theory Concerning a Pre-Adamic Race, p. 16. III. Need for Criticism, p. 42. IV. Variation of Divine Names, p. 42. V. Parallel Stories, p. 91. VI. Unity of Genesis, p. 105.

Archeological Sidelights:

I. Primitive Traditions, p. 59. II. Division of the Nations, p. 64. III. Reflection of Babylonian Life in the Stories of Abraham, p. 76. IV. Reflection of Syrian and Assyrian Life in Stories of Jacob, p. 92. V. Reflection of Egyptian Life in the Joseph Stories, p. 106.

Theological Studies:

I. The Beginning, p. 17. II. God, p. 18. III. Creation, p. 19. IV. Development, p. 19. V. Man, p. 20. VI. Moral Attributes of God, p. 42. VII. Life, p. 44. VIII. Sin, p. 45. IX. Death, p. 46. X. Salvation, p. 46. XI. Worship, p. 55. XII. Effects of Sin, p. 59. XIII. Promises to Abraham, p. 76. XIV. Faith of Abraham, p. 78.

XV. Covenant with Abraham, p. 81. XVI. Chastisement, p. 92. XVII. Election, p. 93. XVIII. Vicarious Suffering, p. 107. XIX. Messiah, p. 107.

EXODUS

Introduction 110

General Outline 111

Detailed Outlines with Textual Notes:
>   Ex. 1:1 to 7:7, p. 112; Ex. 7:8 to 18:27, p. 123; Ex. 19:1 to 24:18, p. 133; Ex. 25:1 to 31:18, p. 145; Ex. 32:1 to 34:35, p. 151; Ex. 35:1 to 40:38, p. 169.

Critical Problems:
>   VII. The Meaning of Ex. 6:2, p. 122. VIII. Chronology of the Exodus, p. 130. IX. Authorship of the Book of the Covenant, p. 141. X. Introduction of Israel to JHWH Worship, p. 142. XI. Relation of the Tabernacle to Israelitic History, p. 150. XII. Contradictions in the Account of Moses' Intercessions, p. 166. XIII. Unity of Exodus, p. 170.

Archeological Sidelights:
>   VI. Pithom and Raamses, p. 123. VII. The Time of the Exodus, p. 130. VIII. Excellence of the Mosaic Law, p. 142. IX. Excellence of the Mosaic Ritual, p. 151.

Theological Studies:
>   XX. Hardening of Pharaoh's Heart, p. 131. XXI. Works of Wonder, p. 131. XXII. Passover, p. 132. XXIII. Covenant Assurances, p. 143. XXIV. Angel of the Covenant, p. 145. XXV. Atonement, p. 151. XXVI. Lessons from the Name, p. 167. XXVII. Means of Revealing the Nature of God, p. 170.

The textbooks are the American Standard Edition of the Bible and this volume. The biblical text serves as the basis for all work, and this volume as a syllabus.

Quotations from Scripture, unless otherwise noted, are from the American Standard Version.

The inspiration and advice of many teachers and friends have contributed to this work in ways too numerous to mention. Two co-workers have rendered valuable aid in the preparation of copy: Rev. J. Hardee Kennedy and Rev. Jesse L. Boyd, Jr.

J. WASH WATTS

New Orleans, Louisiana

LEVITICUS

Introduction 172

Outline and Textual Notes 172

Critical Problems:
XIV. Unity of Leviticus, p. 176.

Archeological Sidelights:
X. Comparison of Gentile Sacrifices with Levitical, p. 177.

NUMBERS

Introduction 178

Outline and Textual Notes 178

Critical Problems:
XV. Unity of Numbers, p. 189.

Archeological Sidelights:
XI. Lack of Monuments Attesting the Wilderness Wanderings, p. 189.

Theological Studies:
XXVIII. Apostasy, p. 190.

DEUTERONOMY

Introduction 191

Outline and Textual Notes 192

Critical Problems:
XVI. Unity of Deuteronomy, p. 205. XVII. Authorship of the Pentateuch, p. 206.

Archeological Sidelights:
XXIX. Possession of Promised Land, p. 208. XXX. Ethical Monotheism, p. 208.

JOB

Introduction 211

Outline and Textual Notes 213

Theological Studies:

> XXXI. Crises in the Experience of Job, p. 227. XXXII. Character of Satan, p. 230. XXXIII. New View of Suffering, p. 230. XXXIV. Distinctions in Sheol, p. 231.

JOSHUA

Introduction 233

Outline and Textual Notes 234

Theological Studies:

> XXXV. Salvation of Rahab, p. 236. XXXVI. Sacredness of the Tribal and Family Allotments, p. 236.

JUDGES

Introduction 238

Outline and Textual Notes 238

Critical Problems:

> XVIII. Dates and Figures in Judges, p. 240.

Theological Studies:

> XXXVII. God's Use of Men with Many Faults, p. 241. XXXVIII. Dan's Departure from His Inheritance, p. 242.

RUTH

Introduction 243

Outline 243

Theological Studies:

> XXXIX. The Bitter-Sweet of Naomi's Experience, p. 244.

SAMUEL

Introduction 246

Outline 247

Theological Studies:

> XL. Meaning of the Kingdom, p. 251. XLI.
> The Anointed of JHWH, p. 253. XLII. The
> Servant of JHWH, p. 254.

PSALMS

Introduction: 256

Outlines:

> List of Studies in Selected Psalms, p. 260; Out-
> line of Psalm 1, p. 261; Psalm 2, p. 266; Psalm
> 18, p. 269; Psalm 22, p. 275; Psalm 23, p. 278;
> Psalm 29, p. 280; Psalm 32, p. 282; Psalm 51,
> p. 283; Psalm 67, p. 286; Psalm 72, p. 289;
> Psalm 73, p. 291; Psalm 103, p. 294; Psalm 110,
> p. 297.

Theological Studies:

> XLIII. Meaning of Blessed, p. 262. XLIV. Na-
> ture, Identity, and Destiny of the Blessed, p.
> 263. XLV. Nature, Identity, and Destiny of the
> Wicked, p. 264. XLVI. The Implications of
> Messianic Control of the Nations, p. 266.
> XLVII. Vengeance in Psalms, p. 270. XLVIII.
> Victory over the Fear of Death, p. 277. XLIX.
> Comfort of the Shepherd's Rod and Staff, p.
> 279. L. The Peace of JHWH Worshipers, p.
> 281. LI. Forgiveness Is JHWH's Assurance of
> Preservation, p. 282. LII. Forgiveness Is As-
> surance of an Answer to Every Prayer, p. 284.
> LIII. Forgiveness Is a Compelling Reason for
> Sharing Salvation, p. 286. LIV. Divine Pro-
> vision for a succession of Rulers, p. 289. LV.
> Antidotes for Pessimism, p. 292. LVI. How Does
> Man Bless God?, p. 295. LVII. Liberty in
> Christ, p. 297.

ABBREVIATIONS FOR WORKS FREQUENTLY USED

MT—Massoretic Text of the Hebrew Old Testament

MTG—Massoretic Text compiled by C. D. Ginsburg

MTK—Massoretic Text arranged by Rud. Kittel in *Biblia Hebraica*

LXX—*The Septuagint*, first translation of the Old Testament, in Greek, made by Jews in Egypt about 275-150 B.C.

Vul—*The Vulgate*, official translation of the Roman Catholic Church, in Latin, made by Jerome about A.D. 390-405

DV—*Douay Version*, English translation of the Vulgate, made in England in A.D. 1609

AV—*Authorized Version*, English translation authorized by King James I of England in A.D. 1611

ERV—*English Revised Version*, made in England by a group of scholars gathered from all Protestant denominations, published in A.D. 1885

ASV—*American Standard Version*, made in America by a group of scholars from all Protestant denominations, published in A.D. 1901

MNT—*A New Translation* by James Moffatt, published in 1922

AT—*An American Translation* by J. M. Powis Smith and a group of scholars, published in 1927

SBD—*Smith's Bible Dictionary*

HDB—*Hasting's Dictionary of the Bible*

ISBE—*International Standard Bible Encyclopaedia*

LOT—*Introduction to the Literature of the Old Testament*, by S. R. Driver

POT—*The Problem of the Old Testament*, by James Orr

MOT—*The Monuments and the Old Testament*, by Ira M. Price

BB—*Biblical Backgrounds*, by J. McKee Adams

HTE—*His Truth Endureth*, by James C. Muir

OTTO—*Old Testament Theology*, by Gustav F. Oehler

OTTS—*Old Testament Theology*, by Herman Schultz

TOT—*Theology of the Old Testament*, by A. B. Davidson

TS—*Typology of Scripture*, by Patrick Fairbairn

CB—*Cambridge Bible for Schools and Colleges*

CC—*Calvin's Commentary*

EB—*The Expositor's Bible*

ICC—*International Critical Commentary*

CPC—*Clarke's People's Commentary*

AC—*The American Commentary*

BC—*The Bible Commentary*

PC—*The Pulpit Commentary*

HC—*The Homiletical Commentary*

CWB—*A Commentary on the Whole Bible*, by Matthew Henry

IEB—*An Interpretation of the English Bible*, by B. H. Carroll

CHS—*A Commentary on the Holy Scriptures*, by Peter Lange

PB—*The People's Commentary*, by Joseph Parker

EHS—*Expositions of Holy Scriptures*, by Alexander Maclaren

INTRODUCTION TO GENESIS

Parallel Reading

Moller, Wilhelm, "Genesis," ISBE
Ryle, H. E., "Genesis," HDB
Conant, Thomas J., "Genesis," SBD
Driver, S. R., "Genesis," LOT
Goodspeed, Calvin, "Introduction," AC

Name and Theme

The first word of the book of Genesis has been used by the Jews as a name for it. In English it means "in beginning." Genesis has been used by Gentile versions from the time of the Septuagint.

Neither of these common names indicates the theme. "In beginning" was not intended to do so. Many think that Genesis was intended to represent the key word of the book, which is "generations." However, generations means things brought forth, or productions, while Genesis means origin, source, or beginning. Thus Genesis fits only the story of beginnings in 1:1 to 2:3. The theme of the book as a whole is the story of early generations.

Authorship and Date

Moses was considered the author of the entire Pentateuch by both Jews and Christians until comparatively recent times. In the eighteenth and nineteenth centuries documentary theories concerning authorship, leading in many cases to denial of Mosaic authorship, gained a wide following among students of these matters. These theories demand painstaking examination of a great amount of evidence. Because of the time and discriminating care

[1]

required, such an examination should be undertaken gradually. Meanwhile it is fair to approach the matter with an open mind and face the facts, no matter to what conclusion they point.

The problem of date is linked with that of authorship and must be examined in the same way.

Plan and Purpose

Evidences of a carefully wrought plan appear in Genesis. The story of the Beginning, leading to the creation of man, is used as an introduction. After that ten major divisions appear, each headed by the word "generations." Thus the meaning of creation, the meaning of generations, and the relation of these two become matters of supreme concern.

The story of the Beginning describes each creation as an act of God, and God alone. Things appear to be brought into being by his creative acts.

The story of the Beginning also describes God as willing the development of each kind of creation according to the possibilities planted in it by his creative act. Original matter is called upon to develop the order and glory of the physical universe. Living creatures are called upon to swarm in the sea, fly in the air, and live on the land. Mankind is called upon to have dominion over all creation.

The story of the Beginning furthermore describes the development of those creations other than man as having come to maturity and as being good in God's sight.

Thus the story of creation gives peculiar prominence to the fact that creation of man in the image of God made possible his dominion over all creation, but it leaves the development of that dominion untold. This is strikingly said in its last verse, "And God blessed the seventh day, . . . because that in it he rested from all his work which God had created for making" (Gen. 2:3). We have lost the significance of the last words, "for making," because our translations have put "and made" in the place of "for making." The change is unjustified; and the loss incurred because of it is serious, for it causes many to lose sight of the fact that creation is simply a prelude to the developments called generations. "For making" means for development, growth, and production. This is the development and production described afterward by the word "generations." The generations are both the physical and the spiritual developments of mankind for which God was waiting when he rested.

The story of early generations then proceeds to picture the ways by which JHWH[1] God assures fulfilment of his purpose for mankind. The first division which deals with the generations of the heavens and the earth, shows bad results. Whereas the developments of all other kinds of creation had been good, man used his free moral agency to choose the fruit of the tree of the knowledge of good and evil; and sin and death followed. However, the danger of sin and death led some men to call upon the name

---

[1]JHWH stands for Jehovah or Yahweh. A discussion of the name appears among the textual notes on Gen. 2:4.

of JHWH; and they are assured of salvation. From there on the development of JHWH worship is the heart of all the stories. Those generations which lead men to JHWH are magnified, and those which turn men from him are discredited. Those of Cain and Esau develop moral decay and ruin. Those of Seth, Noah, Abraham, Isaac, and Jacob are watched over by JHWH so as to remove evil and establish good. The promised seed are assured that they will become a blessing to all mankind and thus fulfil the purpose of God for mankind.

Evidently, the purpose of the book is to tell the story of early generations so as to reveal the salvation provided by JHWH worship.

The general outline built around the word "generations" is as follows:

GENERAL OUTLINE

Theme: Story of Early Generations

Int. The Beginning....................1:1-23

A. Generations of the heavens and the earth .... 2:4 to 4:26

B. Generations of Adam............5:1 to 6:8

C. Generations of Noah...........6:9 to 9:8

D. Generations of the sons of Noah.10:1 to 11:9

E. Generations of Shem..............11:10-26

F. Generations of Terah........11:27 to 25:11

G. Generations of Ishmael...........25:12-18

H. Generations of Isaac........25:19 to 35:29

I. Generations of Esau 36:1-43

J. Generations of Jacob........37:1 to 50:26

DETAILED OUTLINE

Theme: The Beginning

I

Creation and Development of the Heavens and the Earth

1. Creation by God........................1:1

2. Creation in a chaotic (unordered) state....1:2a

3. Brooded over by the Spirit of God........1:2b

4. Development of light...................1:3-5

5. Development of the firmament (expanse).1:6-8

6. Development of land and sea..........1:9-13

7. Development of heavenly bodies......1:14-19

II

Creation and Early Development of Living Creatures

1. God's will for development first in the sea and air 1:20

2. Creation after their kind in the sea and air.1:21

3. Command to multiply................1:22-23

4. Development of land creatures........1:24-25

III

Creation of Mankind

1. God's will for development after the likeness of God 1:26

2. Creation in the image of God............1:27

3. Command to multiply and have dominion over all creation....................1:28-31

Conclusion

God's rest from creation, awaiting development of his creatures 2:1-3

TEXTUAL NOTES

1:1. The Hebrew word for God is *Elohim*. It probably means the All-Powerful. The word is plural but is used with a singular verb. Hebrew plurals are often used to indicate fulness or completeness. In this sense the plural subject indicates the plenitude of God's power. In any case the singular verb indicates that the subject is one in the sense of being perfectly unified.

"Create" appears to mean bring into being. The absence of any mention of pre-existing material indicates that and warrants this New Testament interpretation, "By faith we understand that the worlds have been framed by the word of God, so that what is seen hath not been made out of things which appear" (Heb. 11:3).

1:2. "Brooding" is a far better translation than "moving" (Cf. footnote of ASV). Brooding gives a perfect picture of the influence of the Spirit of God upon original matter so as to bring forth its inherent possibilities, as the brooding of a hen develops the inherent possibilities in her eggs.

1:3. "Let there be" expresses desire, expectation, and will that the thing referred to will come to pass, but also that it will be caused to do so by some other power than that of the speaker. If one says, Let the door be shut, he expects someone else to shut it. Thus, when God said, "Let there be light," he called upon inherent forces in original matter to generate light. This is development and not creation. Many similar expressions scattered through the story of the beginning call for development. (Cf. 1:6, 9, 11, 14, 20, 24).

1:4. "It was good" describes light, the first production of original matter. Whenever used this description indicates God's approval of things developed out of his creations. (Cf. 1:12, 18, 21, 25, 31).

1:5. The word "day" is used at other places in the Bible to describe a period of time other than the twenty-four hour day. (Cf. Job 14:6). There appears to be no reason why it could not do so here. (Cf. 1:8, 13, 19, 23, 31). Moreover, the fact that the day described in 2:2-3 is not described as coming to a close appears to lead to the conclusion that it does do so here.

1:7. "Made" is used to describe God's part in the developments. In other words, whenever God made

something, he used pre-existing material and inter-
mediate causes. That is development, not creation.
(Cf. 1:16, 25-26; 2:2-3).

"It was so" is another statement used to indicate
fulfilment of God's will concerning development.
(Cf. 1:9, 11, 15, 24, 30). "It was good" and "It was
so" together mark all the developments willed by
God as fulfilled in accord with his will, except man's
use of his moral and spiritual nature so as to exercise dominion over creation after the likeness of God.

1:20. "Living creatures" is literally "living
souls." The word for soul primarily means that
which breathes, so this kind of soul is indicated as
belonging to all that breathe. It distinguishes the
animate from the inanimate and is endowed with the
faculties of sensation, consciousness, and voluntary
motion.

1:21. "Created" is used for the second time. It
appears to be linked with the distinctive faculties
of the living creatures, making the statement of 1:24,
"Let the earth bring forth living creatures," to refer
to the development of their bodies.

1:24-25. The living creatures of the land are
not said to have been created but made. The in-
ference is that they were developed from other creatures.

1:26. "Let us make" is exceedingly interesting
in every word.

"Let" expresses another appeal, similar to the
other appeals in this story for co-operation of other

powers. Thus it is associated hitherto only with plans for development.

"Us" accords with the plural form of God. Many have sought to explain this fact as a royal manner of speech, wherein a monarch describes his word as the word of himself and his people, though he alone is the author. Others have thought that angels were thus appealed to for their co-operation. However, the correspondence with the plural form of the name God seems to make it more reasonable to suppose that an appeal to the other members of the Godhead was intended.

"Make" accords both with the "let" and the "us." It accords with "let" in indicating that the purpose of God for man includes development. Man's body is developed from pre-existing material. Moreover, man is not expected to start full grown. It accords with "us" in that it is plural, being the only plural verb used with God in the story. It prepares us to expect that the development of man will be promoted in a way that will utilize all the persons of the Godhead. The added fact that this is brought out only in connection with mankind places a supreme emphasis upon the interest of God in the development of man.

"Man" comes from the same root as the word ground and describes human beings as to their earthly origin, made "of the dust."

"Image" and "likeness" have essentially the same meaning. An image is something that is cut out so as to be like something else. Thus image here is that wherein man is like God and God like man, that which is common to both. It cannot refer to man's physical nature, as God is Spirit. It can refer only to the spiritual and moral nature of man, including his intellectual, emotional, and volitional faculties, the distinctive features of spiritual personality. These faculties distinguish man from all other creatures and make him like God.

"Dominion" is made the goal of man's development. His distinctive faculties, intellect, emotion, and will power, fit him to rule creation, if only he can rule himself.

1:27. "Created" brings before us the third and last creative act mentioned in the story of creation. The word "created" is used here three times, but all three uses refer to the same act. The second use emphasizes the fact that it was "in the image of God" that man was created. The third use emphasizes that man here is mankind, including man and woman.

The emphasis upon the creation of man in God's image emphasizes both the supreme worth of the image of God and the fact that man's creation applies to the distinctive faculties of that image, not the development of the body. (Cf. Gen. 2:5-7).

1:28. The command, "Be fruitful and multiply," shows that propagation of the race was a part of God's purpose for mankind from the beginning. This implies that it is not the result of sin.

"Replenish" ought to be translated "fill." The Hebrew verb used can refer to the first act of filling as well as any other. When there is no occasion for thinking that the filling referred to is not the first, it should be translated "fill." The same verb, used in exactly the same way in 1:22, is translated "fill."

1:29-30. The provision for food indicated here shows that it was not according to the original purpose of God to permit the taking of life in order to provide food for man or beast.

2:1. "Finished" is used only of the "heavens and the earth," the first of God's creations. This indicates that God's development of the heavens and the earth had come to a state of completion in the time of the beginning, but not so with animals and men.

2:2. God's rest is described as bringing to a halt God's activity, both of creation and development. This seems to require the understanding that creation, and such developments as required more than the independent development of possibilities already established by creation, ceased, but that such independent developments were not brought to a halt. At least the omission of animals and men from the statements of 2:1 indicates that their development was not complete. Being endowed with ability to develop independently, in accord with the commands of 1:22 and 1:28, their development was not halted.

2:3. "Hallowed it" means set it apart unto the use of God. This setting apart of a seventh of time unto the use of God is what is declared blessed.

"Which God had created and made" ought to be translated "which God had created for making." There appears to be no justification for the substitution made in our translation. The Septuagint made an attempt to stay close to the original by saying, "Which God began to make." The Vulgate shifted over to the translation copied by our English versions. Maybe Jerome failed to see the relation of creation to development, so artfully indicated by the story of creation and so fittingly expressed by a literal translation of these last words. His translation hinders our understanding of the story of the Beginning in two ways: (1) It indicates that making or development refers only to what had been completed within this period of creation; (2) it obscures the statement that God's purpose for the things he has created is development. "Created for making," with its context, of course, says that the creation, which God and God alone could accomplish, was finished; but that God's highest creatures, animals and men, were intended for developments which were only begun. As original matter under the brooding of the Spirit of God had already developed into an orderly universe, so should the higher creations develop the possibilities of perfection planted in them by God's creation of them. The unfolding, the ruining, the salvation of these possibilities of perfection, in man particularly, is the theme of Genesis and of the Bible.

CRITICAL PROBLEMS

I

The Stories of Genesis

The story of the Beginning furnishes an example of the stories that make up the book of Genesis. We may, therefore, observe even at the beginning that the literary form of the book is that of a great historical and religious story.

These stories magnify the early heroes of the human race. To that extent they are like folklore. However, folklore is a loose collection of stories that have arisen from a people without the unifying interpretation of a great author or editor to give consistency, truth, and greatness to the message as a whole. Therefore, the message of folklore is frequently spoiled by fictitious characters and experiences, the ideals of mythology, ancestor worship, and the ungodly glorifying of human heroes. These stories are skilfully blended into one great story by the hand of a master at storytelling. This great story frankly pictures the good and the bad in its heroes, and appraises them as worthy of enduring honor only when they recognize JHWH God as the source of their blessings. Thus Genesis brings a truly great religious message in story form.

These stories give a connected account of several thousand years of early human development. To that extent they are history. However, ordinary history tries to give a full chronicle of events, no matter whether dull or interesting, no matter whether disconnected or unified. These stories select for interpretation certain facts of history pertaining to the one central message concerning the power of JHWH to save men from sin. They vivify, dramatize, and give to those facts all the colorful interpretation which the art of storytelling can command. By this inspiration they bring out of those facts a revelation of salvation.

These stories offer an explanation of certain laws that operate in physical nature. To that extent they overlap the sphere of physical science. However, physical science makes no attempt to explain the power that brought nature into being, because it finds no physical cause back of nature, and it has no place for a spiritual cause like God. It deals with creation, not with the creator. Moreover, physical science has no place for other contacts between a supreme spiritual power and physical nature, as in the case of miracles like the appearance of God as the Angel of JHWH to human eyes, and in the case of regeneration of the human soul when it looks to JHWH for redemption from sin. No wonder then that the treatment of physical nature in these stories is different from that of a physical science! They do not contradict the facts of physical science, but they rise to higher truths than those perceived by the physical senses alone. By means of a skill that makes the men of old to relive their lowest and their highest experiences before our eyes, these stories make God and faith to be the truths that are supremely important.

order which gradually developed. The story that follows shows that it was God's will for cosmic order to be a development rather than a feature of original matter.

As shown already (cf. note on 1:22), the "replenish" of 1:22 should be "fill." This is important because advocates of this theory have seized upon this verse in order to claim that "replenish" implied that the earth had previously been full and then emptied according to their theory.

There is literally nothing in the story of the Beginning to furnish a basis for this theory.

The story of the Beginning does give its supreme emphasis to the teaching that God made the earth and all that is in it for the human race, purposing that man should have dominion over it by reason of the image of God that is in him.

THEOLOGICAL STUDIES

I

The Beginning

The Beginning referred to in Genesis 1:1 is the beginning of creation and so of time. There is only one such beginning. We may therefore translate the first words as "In beginning" or "In the beginning." Either translation must refer to the same thing.

The most important fact about this Beginning as described by the Bible is that it is caused by God, and God alone. This implies that he existed eternally, before any created thing came into being. It states that he is the cause of all creation. We are moved by these simple words toward the supremely important conclusion that "in him all things consist" (Col. 1:17). This conclusion is the foundation for all biblical theology and philosophy.

The fulfilment of the will of God for mankind is the theme of the Bible. This theme distinguishes it from all other books and makes it the Book, the Bible. Christian philosophy may and should make this theme its center. When so, philosophy is simply an expansion of biblical theology, making the revelations of the Bible and the affirmations of biblical faith foundations for its reasoning. When philosophy attempts to exclude these from its foundations, it ceases to be biblical in its viewpoint. Thus the Bible remains the Book for all men of faith.

II

God

God is portrayed, either by statements or implication, as being:

1. Eternal. He existed before the beginning of time.

2. Omnipotent. The name God indicates plenitude of power. The power to create and develop is of him.

3. Personal. He has knowledge, desire, and will. He makes man in his image and thereby endows him with the faculties of personality.

2. Consequences declared by JHWH God....3:9-21
Int. Confession and excuse
       of Adam and Eve............3:9-13

(1) For the serpent, a curse: warfare begun by the woman and
ending in victory for her seed...3:14-15

(2) For the woman, multiplication
of pain and conception and subjection to her husband...........3:16

(3) For the man, lifelong toil......3:17-19
Con. JHWH God provides clothing
by killing animals.............3:20-21

III

Man's Death

1. Loss of eternal life 3:22-24
2. Hypocrisy in worship...................4:1-7
3. Manslaughter 4:8
4. Wavering and wandering..............4:9-16
5. Polygamy, murder, and defiance of
    justice 4:17-24

Con. Line of Seth seeks salvation by
worship of JHWH...................4:25-26

TEXTUAL NOTES

Generations

2:4 introduces the word "generations."

"The generations of the heavens and the earth"
are things brought forth by them. These are de-

scribed as being: (1) man's opportunity for moral dominion; (2) man's sin; (3) man's spiritual death. Accordingly, these generations include more than the material productions of the heavens and the earth. They include the moral test and effects involved in the use of the material productions; in other words, man's spiritual experiences.

The fact that this first heading covers man's sin and man's spiritual death is proof that the time clause, "When they were created, in the day that Jehovah God made earth and heaven," ought not to be attached to it. Man's sin and spiritual death came after the making of earth and heaven. Therefore, this time clause should be attached to what follows, and the heading left as a heading only, as is done in Genesis 5:1.

Since this word "generations" always refers to productions or developments, it is a violation of it to translate it as "origins" after the fashion of AT, or to make it cover the acts of creation by moving it to Genesis 1:1 after the fashion of MNT.

.   .   .   .

JHWH God

"Jehovah God" is a new name for God introduced in 2:4. The second member of this compound name in its original form is the *Elohim* of the story of the Beginning. It is the generic name for God and at this point tells us that this is the same God that was in the story of the Beginning. The first member, however, gives a proper name.

In Old Testament times, proper names were given as descriptions of character; so we may expect this one to bring some description of God's personal character. It is left, however, largely to later Scriptures to indicate what this description of the personal character of God is. They must be studied as we come to them.

This matter of the personal name for God is obviously too great a matter to be comprehended all at once. The one pertinent fact that is noticeable here is that the name is introduced as soon as we enter the story that deals exclusively with mankind. The Bible devotes one brief story only to the universe in general, all else to mankind. What an emphasis upon the value of the personality of mankind! This description of the personal God is immediately interwoven with the special account of humanity's struggles and destiny. It is artfully brought in, as a master storyteller introduces gently, gradually, and frequently those great things upon which he would concentrate a natural and eager interest, in order that the exposition of its greatness be not missed when it comes.

The translation of the original form of this personal name has occasioned an unending amount of discussion. There is no hope of unanimity of opinion concerning it. Because early Hebrew was written without vowels, all certainty as to its full form has been lost. The one thing certain is that only the consonants of the original word appear in the Hebrew text. When transliterated they are usually given as JHWH. This transliteration, the only certain form of this word that is known, will be used in our studies, leaving each student to choose for himself his way of handling it. Outstanding ways of handling it have included transliteration of the four consonants which have come down to us, substitution of the word Lord for the original, mixture of the original consonants with the vowels for Lord, and scholarly guesses as to the complete original word. More complete explanations are as follows:

1. The Jewish way. Because Jews came to think of this name as too sacred for anyone to pronounce, except the high priest on the day of atonement in the Holy of holies, they substituted for it the word *Adhonai*, Lord.

2. The way of the LXX, Vul, AV, and ERV. Following the Jewish custom, these versions have used Lord, each in its own language, of course. The present American Revision Committee has recently decided to forsake the use of "Jehovah" and follow the other versions in using Lord.

3. The way of the ASV. In A.D. 1518, Petrus Galatinus, Confessor of Leo X, suggested that the vowels of the Hebrew word for Lord be read with the consonants of the original word. By this time Hebrew texts included vowels, and those of Lord were written under the consonants of the original word, so that it was an easy way out of difficulties to read them together, though they did make a hybrid word. Because the word thus formed, Jehovah, does at least represent the original as a "personal

name," which "designates God as the personal God, as the covenant God, the God of revelation, the Deliverer, the Friend of his people,"[2] the original American Revision Committee adopted it.

4. The way of scholarly guesses concerning the original. These use Yahweh, Jahweh, Yahveh, or Jahveh. All these are approximately the same, and most authors agree in representing the verb to be as the root of the original. Some explain the meaning of the name as arising out of the teaching in Exodus 3:12-15 and indicating the great "I AM," The Eternal; others point to its use in Genesis 4:1 as indicating the Life Giver or He Who Causes to Be; others develop various shades of meaning.

Probably the most important consideration in our choice of a way to handle this word is our need to be reminded that the original was a description of the personal character of God. The use in written language of the *tetragrammaton,* the four original letters, will at least require each reader to make a choice of his own for use in speech, and force upon him perhaps the choice best suited to him individually as a reminder concerning the meaning of "this glorious and fearful name."[3] This will approximate what is done with the Hebrew text, where the four letters appear as originally written; yet each reader must choose for himself his way of speaking the name. Such usage seems to be the nearest approach

[2] Preface to the American Standard Version of the Bible.
[3] Deut. 28:58.

to correct representation of the original that is possible.

.   .   .   .

2:7. The development of man's body is very clearly stated here.

"Breath of life" is literally "breath of lives" or "breath of the fullness of life." This is the created portion of man.

"A living soul" is literally "a soul of lives" or "a soul of the fullness of life."

2:8. Speculation as to the location of the garden of Eden does not help us to see the teaching of these passages and it will therefore be left to other works. The teaching is supremely ethical and spiritual.

2:9. A distinction between the trees in the garden of Eden appears to be indicated by the "also" that follows "the tree of life." This gives two classes of trees, the first including "every tree that is pleasant to the sight and good for food," the second including the "tree of life . . . and the tree of the knowledge of good and evil."

Meaning of the Trees in the Garden of Eden

The trees in the first class are evidently literal trees, but those in the second appear to be figurative.

The first are the ones which all of us see brought forth by the heavens and the earth, when the rain from heaven causes the seed in the earth to sprout. These are literal trees that provide man with pleasure and food. The fact that these are the generations of the heavens and the earth, even as the body of man, is obvious.

Those in the second group bear descriptions that belong to no literal tree but picture moral and spiritual experiences. They also grow up with the other trees, as if to indicate that these experiences develop along with the eating of the fruit of the other trees.

The word for life is the same word used in the expression, "breath of life," in Genesis 2:7. It is also the plural of the word translated "living" in "living soul,"[4] "living creatures,"[5] and "life."[6] The use of the plural appears first in this description of the life of man, is associated afterward almost exclusively with man, and was probably intended here to emphasize the fulness of life given to him. Thus "the tree of life" symbolizes opportunity to experience the fulness of life as a fruitage of dominion over creation.

The word for "knowledge" in this context appears to carry a meaning it frequently bears, which signifies more than intellectual perception, and includes experience. Thus "knowledge of good and evil" means experience of both good and evil. Accordingly, "the tree of the knowledge of good and evil" symbolizes the fact that the spiritual life with which God endowed man involves possible knowledge of good and evil as soon as he begins to use the other trees in the garden. In turn, the words, "in the day that thou eatest thereof thou shalt surely

---

[4]Gen. 2:7.   [5]Gen. 1:20.   [6]Gen. 1:30.

die," show that death refers to the destruction of that spiritual life with which God had endowed him.

This is a beautifully fitting picture of the moral issue raised for man as soon as he exercises his dominion over creation. Control of possessions by a human soul inevitably involves moral responsibility. Thus moral developments are also generations of the heavens and the earth. In the wisdom of God this issue has been made to be the experience of every normal human as soon as spiritual and moral consciousness awakes. Its fundamental importance makes it the theme of the first story in the epic of man's spiritual experience.

.   .   .   .

2:15. "To keep it" means more than "to dress it." It means to guard it or keep it as God had created it and intended it—good, only good!

2:16-17. God's commands are very emphatic.

The first emphasizes the fact that it was God's desire for man to eat of all the trees in the garden of Eden except the tree of the knowledge of good and evil. Therefore, his desire included the tree of life. The fulness of life was to be a development of man's life, if he would heed the commands of God.

The second command emphasizes the fact that knowledge of both good and evil was possible, but contrary to the will of God, and therefore deadly.

Together these commands emphasize the fact that the result of man's exercise of his moral freedom and will power will be either life or death. The issue depends upon his determination to obey or not to obey.

2:18. "Help meet for him" means "a help corresponding to him; i. e., equal and adequate to himself."[7] Woman corresponds to man in two ways, both being of vital importance to his happiness and success. First, she corresponds in the sense of being equal, being developed from the same kind as he (Cf. 2:21-23), and being on the same level spiritually and morally. She alone from among the living creatures could so correspond, for she was the only other creature made in the image of God. In the second place, she corresponds in the sense that opposites correspond, that of meeting his need, even as he meets hers, so that the two complement each other. This correspondence is beautifully expressed in the saying that she was "not made out of his head to rule him; nor out of his feet to be trampled on by him; but out of his side to be equal to him; under his arm to be protected; and near his heart to be loved by him."[8]

It is significant that this provision for a helpmeet and a home is given as a completing step in God's preparation of man for his efforts to rule over creation. To abandon God's ideals for the home is to abandon man's finest aid in the struggle of life aside from God himself.

2:24. God's provision of one woman for one man was accepted spontaneously by man as a moral ideal

[7]Brown, Driver, and Briggs, *Hebrew and English Lexicon*, p. 617.
[8]Quoted by Sampey, John R., *Heart of the Old Testament*, p. 20.

for the home. So must monogamy appeal to any conscience yet innocent and uncompromised by sin. (Cf. Matt. 19:3-9.)

2:25. Nakedness without shame is pointed out here as evidence of innocence. The body is not shameful, for God made it. Sinful use of it causes a sense of shame concerning it, but neither sin nor shame was present in the beginning. Man's life, including home life, was established in innocence.

3:1. "The serpent" is placed emphatically here. There is sharp contrast between this use of emphasis and that in 2:4-25, for there it was upon JHWH God. This marks the serpent as the author of sin. (Cf. James 1:13.)

The identity of the serpent is very clearly stated in the Revelation 20:2, "the dragon, the old serpent, which is the Devil and Satan."

"Subtle" means crafty, shrewd. The insinuating nature of the serpent's temptations reveals the reason for his appearance as the serpent and the description of him as subtle. Shrewdness manifests intelligence, but it is such intelligence as can be prostituted to evil purposes. Craftiness manifests skill and art, but it is such art as may be deceitful and destructive. The final effect appears from the root idea of the word, which is to strip as flesh from bone, and lay bare as a tree without bark or leaves. All these phases of meaning are peculiarly applicable to the work of the tempter.

The work of the tempter begins here with a question, not an honest request for information, but an insinuating question intended to indicate that something is wrong. All temptation begins this way. Such questions lead to doubt, forbidden desires, and disobedience.

3:2. "The fruit of the tree" is the fruit of the tree of the knowledge of good and evil. If that tree is symbolical, its fruit is symbolical. We should not think then of the fruit as describing a particular act but all kinds of sinful acts. We run into subtle difficulty when we make this literal and apply it to some particular act. The person not tempted to do that particular thing then fails to see that this story applies just as forcefully to him as to others. Symbolically interpreted, it applies to every temptation.

3:4. The serpent's assertion, "Ye shall not surely die," may have led Eve to think only of physical death. Physical death is hastened by sin, but does not necessarily come immediately. Any confusion of thought concerning God's meaning fits the purpose of the tempter and breeds distrust of God's Word.

3:5-6. "Ye shall be as God, knowing good and evil," is another subtle, devilish lie. It has just enough truth in it to deceive the heart attracted by desire for the knowledge to which it refers.

This knowledge is experiential knowledge in man's case but not in God's. Man, innocent and limited in knowledge, cannot gain understanding of the nature and blessing of good or the nature and curse of sin except through experience. God, perfect and unlimited in any way, has understanding of these things without the experience of evil doing.

To such extent as man may gain understanding of the nature and curse of sin, to that extent he becomes like God by sinning. And that possibility has tremendous attraction for human hearts. They see that the experience has in it certain possibilities for the acquirement of "food" or physical satisfaction, for "a delight to the eyes" or a psychic thrill, and for making one "wise" or imparting the intellectual shrewdness that succeeds in doing what one wants to do. This much of the tempter's picture of sin is true.

However, the subtle impression that man may gain this understanding of the nature and curse of sin and yet be as God in possession of goodness and fulness of life is a cruel, fatal deception.

This wicked suggestion was skilfully calculated to cause doubt of God's love and God's desire to give man his best.

The act of disobedience to which this suggestion led was an expression of doubt that God's righteous wrath and retribution would follow.

3:7. Nakedness is here associated with shame. The effort of man and woman to clothe themselves revealed that association in their thinking. This shame is the natural result of yielding to the subtlety of the tempter. His subtlety, however, strips or lays bare the soul of man, not the body. Yet it is the body that shame leads man to cover up. Such is the inconsistency and confusion caused by sin. It is his naked soul which man needs to confess to God rather than trying to hide from him his naked body.

The association of shame by man and woman with their own bodies shows that sin affected their relations with each other. No matter where or how sin originated, it was inevitable that this should develop sooner or later. All that is central and vital in man's life is quickly affected by sin.

3:8. The hiding of themselves from God is the result of their confusion about their nakedness and the right way to cover it. It is typical of sinners. They tried in their own way to cover it, but their efforts did not save them from a sense of guilt and from fear of God; so they tried to escape from God. They separated themselves from his presence; yet he, despite their sin and shame, still sought fellowship with them.

3:12. The man confessed but tried to shift responsibility.

3:13. The woman confessed but tried to shift responsibility.

3:14. God judged the serpent as the author of sin, bearing the primary, chief, and irrevocable responsibility for sin. As one irremediably identified with sin and so reprobate, upon him is placed a curse above or exceeding that upon any other creature.

The curse upon the serpent is a prophecy of his doom. Curses and blessings are parallel in that both are prophecies. This parallel may be observed in Genesis 12:3; 27:29; Numbers 22:6, 12; 23:7; 24:9. Thus the curse does not condemn the serpent to immediate destruction, but it does assure his ultimate destruction. Thus it is a prophecy to be treasured by mankind, to give warning to all who would continue to follow him, but hope to all who would resist him. This prophecy is a companion piece to the one that follows concerning victory over sin for the seed of the woman.

3:15. "Enmity" is hostility to a personal foe. As God first said he would put enmity between the serpent and the woman, we have here a prophecy that the warfare against Satan would be begun by her. She who first succumbed to temptation would first resist the power of the tempter.

"Thy seed and her seed" must refer to spiritual seed, those who continue this spiritual enmity or warfare between the serpent and the woman. The seed of the serpent could not be physical seed.

Seed is a collective noun like people, which can be considered either singular or plural. This gives rise to the possibility of fulfilment of the promise concerning the seed of the woman in a single seed and in a numerous seed. Those who see in the prophecy prediction concerning a people who will be victorious over sin and Satan are not wrong, provided they do not contradict the revelations of later Scriptures concerning the necessity for a savior able to save this people, a savior through whom, and through whom alone, this people can win their victory. Those who see in this prophecy prediction foreshadowing the Christ are not wrong, if they can also admit the other. Paul in Galatians 3:16 was not contradicting the first interpretation but adding the second. Christ is certainly essential to the fulfilment of the prophecy, but that was doubtless not seen at the time it was given.

The contrast between "head" and "heel" indicates that both sides are to suffer in the warfare, but the fatal wounds are for the serpent, and the victory for the seed of the woman.

The First Evangel

This prophecy of victory is a ground for human hope. Enduring hope is essential to ultimate victory. Without hope, the suffering in the midst of warfare would doubtless crush all. Doubtless God made these first prophecies of Genesis 3:14-15 to be his first pronouncements upon sin that no suffering sinner need ever be overwhelmed by despair. They are the beginning of the gospel.

. . . .

3:16. The woman is made to bear responsibility for her sin. The consequences, however, should not be misinterpreted. They include multiplication of pain and conception but not normal conception and consequent pain. They include subjection to her husband, whenever the disorder introduced by sin into home or society makes subjection of one to another necessary to the maintenance of order, but not when the love that is in Christ has removed sin and disorder so that husband and wife are the harmonious complements of each other that God originally purposed them to be.

3:17. The man is made to bear his responsibility. Again we need to take great care not to misinterpret the consequences. They include toil, the pain or sorrow attendant upon difficulties, but not such labor as was contemplated in 2:15. They include lifelong subjection to hardship in making a living but not physical death. The statement, "Dust thou art and unto dust shall thou return," is given in explanation of the preceding clause, "Till thou return unto the ground," but not of the judgment resting upon man during that time. That return to the dust is assumed as inevitable for the body, sooner or later, regardless of sin. But that return need not have been attended by travail and grief had man not sinned.

3:21. God's provision of durable clothing, following the development of sin and shame, reflects recognition of a need for clothes. Moreover, his use of animals for this purpose gives approval of their use for worthy purposes.

The idea that this was also an example of bloody sacrifice is not warranted by anything in this text.

3:24. "The Cherubim" appear to belong to the list of symbolical characters we find in these early stories. To realize what they symbolize we need to note the following facts: (1) 3:22 recounts, immediately after man's fall, the purpose of JHWH God

to deprive man of the fruit of the tree of life, in
other words, of life eternal; (2) 3:23 recounts the
act of deprivation; (3) 3:24 evidently gives the
symbol of that deprivation. Thus the Cherubim
"keep the way" to eternal life or full fellowship with
God. Their association with the presence of God
corresponds with their use elsewhere; in the tabernacle and the Temple, especially in connection with
the holy of holies, the ark, and the mercy seat; in
Isaiah's vision of God, where the Seraphim are very
probably to be identified with the Cherubim (Isa.
chap. 6); in the visions of Ezekiel, by the River Che-
bar, and at Jerusalem (Ezek. 1:8-11); and in
the vision of John, where they are called "living
creatures" (Rev. 4). We need to observe also, "the
flame of a sword which turned every way." The
association of the Cherubim with this flame is
peculiar to this passage and must be interpreted in
the light of the immediate context. The two together symbolize the deprivation already purposed
and enforced; they symbolize it as a penalty for sin,
"flame" and "sword" being connected naturally with
punishment; they symbolize it as inflicted upon the
whole race, "turning every way" to face every man.

4:1. The name Cain appears to mean One Built
or Produced, as manufactured goods are fabricated.
Eve made a play upon his name, using a verb similar
in spelling and said, "I have gotten a man with the
help of JHWH."

"With JHWH" indicates recognition by Eve of
the distinction made in the preceding Scriptures con-

cerning the development of man's body and the creation of his soul. Eve saw that this acquisition to the family was not merely produced by her but also created by JHWH.

The name Abel is not explained. The word, as used later, means emptiness or vanity. Nothing in Scripture fits the idea of vanity. Only the fact of being killed while yet young seems to have any connection with emptiness. That connection is possible, but it would make the name to be one given after death, and it is entirely a guess.

First Use of JHWH on Human Lips

Eve's use of the name JHWH is given as the first on human lips. Thus its first meaning must be judged in view of her circumstances. These point to the meaning, "He Who Causes to Be" or "Giver of Life."

.   .   .   .

4:5. "His countenance fell" describes a facial expression of Cain's anger. It did not reflect any sense of shame like that of Adam and Eve after their fall, any pain of heart because of guilt, or any effort to understand the reason for rejection of his offering, merely resentment at the fact. That is the way of unconfessing, unrepentant sinners.

4:6. Yet JHWH pleaded with and sought to help such a sinner as Cain.

4:7. The statement, "If thou doest well, shall it not be lifted up," distinguishes Cain's offering from the reason for its rejection. This statement clearly indicates God's willingness to receive his offering in case his conduct is good. His fault, therefore, did not lie in the kind or amount of the offering he brought but in his conduct. His conduct was not in accord with the attitude toward God which an offering is supposed to represent. When one voluntarily brings an offering to another from whom he has been estranged because he has sinned against him, that offering professes to indicate desire for reconciliation, consciousness of guilt, willingness to make amends, prayer for understanding, and renewed friendship. When an offering is not an expression of these attitudes, it is a sham, a bribe upon an altar, an evidence of hypocrisy in worship.

"Sin coucheth" describes sin as waiting like a wild beast for its prey. When a man has begun to play the hypocrite in his dealings with God, he is horribly near to that state in which man can no longer understand or heed the plea, "Do thou rule over it." Unless he does soon heed, the beast will spring as he did upon Cain and proceed to tear and destroy.

4:8. Manslaughter followed for no other reason than jealousy and blind fury born of stubborn sin.

4:9-16. The curse, it needs to be remembered, is a prophecy. It points here to the inevitable consequences of sin that must follow inasmuch as Cain refused to listen to God. Cain is told that he will become a "fugitive," a wavering, trembling one, and a "wanderer." These predictions were fulfilled to such extent that the land in which he dwelt was called Nod, which means Wandering.

4:17-24. The genealogy of Cain's descendants seems to be given chiefly for the purpose of leading up to the sins of Lamech. Despite remarkable brilliancy among the descendants of Cain, bringing development of city life, art, and industry, sin grew worse and worse. Polygamy developed first with Lamech, and he also became a defiant man-killer. His poem admits it and seems to glory in it.

The Lost Line

Here the curtain is drawn over the picture of Cain's line. It is revealed as possessed by the destroying power of sin, then dismissed from the Bible. The Bible goes on with the accounts of the men of faith. Genesis thus deals summarily with all generations that do not remain in the line of promise.

. . . .

4:25. Seth means Appointed One. The meaning probably signifies more than the mere giving of another child. It seems to look back to the promise of "a seed" through which the warfare with the serpent is carried on to victory. Eve had evidently set her hopes upon Abel, because his worship was acceptable. No mention was made of Cain, for he had obviously disqualified himself.

4:26. Enos means Weak One, or Mortal One. The idea of physical weakness does not fit, because we are told in Genesis 5:11 that he lived nine hundred and five years. The idea of mortality, however, thought of the prospect and imminent danger of death, is quite fitting when we observe the prominence given to the threat of manslaughter by the attaching of this word about Enosh to the story of Cain's line. The fear of death must have hung like a cloud over the thinking of each human family by this time. Furthermore, this recognition of the danger of death may have close connection with the development in worship which follows.

First Use of JHWH in Worship

The statement, "Then began men to call upon the name of Jehovah," is connected directly with Enosh. Probably the connection is a more meaningful one than that of mere time. "To call upon" meant to invoke in prayer or worship, as we pray "in the name of Jesus." However, as this worship in the time of Enosh is not the beginning of worship, the important point here is not the fact that men worshiped but that in the name of JHWH they worshiped. This is the first use of JHWH in worship, and the connection with Enosh probably indicates that the fear of death made the meaning of JHWH particularly appealing. If Eve thought of God as Giver-of-Life, it was most natural for Seth and Enosh to think of him as Preserver-of-Life. The derivation of the name from the verb to be and the use of it in the causative form would express both ideas.

CRITICAL PROBLEMS

III

Need for Criticism

Parallel Reading: "Criticism of the Bible," in *ISBE*.

Question for student investigation: Is there any practical aid for Christian workers in biblical criticism?

IV

Variation of Divine Names

Parallel Reading: same as under III (Especially section III-1)

Question for student investigation: Is there any spiritual lesson in the variation of divine names in Genesis 1:1 to 4:26?

THEOLOGICAL STUDIES

VI

Moral Attributes of God

The description of God grows with each story, for he is in all of them. We see in these stories concerning the generations of the heavens and the earth that the attributes of spiritual personality begin to take shape. These stories describe the spiritual relations of God and men, and their dealings of course reflect attributes of character in both. Thus in God we see the following attributes: (1) truth, (2) love,

(3) righteousness. The words are ours, but the characteristics they signify are manifest.

God's truth is manifest in his statements about life and death and their fulfilment.

God's love is manifest in: (1) his desire for man to enjoy the fruit of the tree of life, the fulness of life; (2) his warning against eating of the fruit of the tree of the knowledge of good and evil, in other words, against sin; (3) his tender, considerate, wise, and gracious cultivation of hope by the promise of victory over sin; (4) his provision for the practical needs of man by providing a helpmeet and skins for clothing.

God's righteousness is manifest in: (1) his provision of a moral test for man with life or death depending on the issue; (2) his curse upon the reprobate serpent; (3) his punishment of the guilty, though sorrowful, man and woman.

The appearance of these moral attributes together give the impression that God is faithful to every moral obligation in himself and in man. The association of these with the name JHWH, the personal name for God, is doubtless not without significance. The use of this name from the beginning of this group of stories is the work of the author, not of the characters in them. His reasons do not necessarily appear in full as yet, but it is striking that he used it as soon as he came to the description of man's moral nature and struggle. The name must have special significance for moral beings and their struggle with sin. The first use on human lips and the first use in worship bear this same significance.

VII

Life

Life is described as being: (1) spiritual, (2) eternal, (3) moral, (4) fellowship with God.

The spiritual quality of life is shown by the use of the word. In every case it is used of that which God created, in sharp distinction from everything developed out of matter.

The eternal quality of life appears in the expressions, "breath of life [lives]," and "a living soul [soul of lives]," in Genesis 2:7, along with the treatment of "the tree of life [lives]." These plurals with their context describe a fulness of life for men, the possibility of which inheres in the image of God. The word eternal, meaning unlimited in time or quality, accords with this fulness that belongs to life from God.

The moral quality appears in the choice between the tree of life and the tree of the knowledge of good and evil, between a godlike life of good alone and experience of both good and evil. The choice involves discrimination between good and evil. The choice is a free, individual exercise of man's faculties of intelligence, love, and will power. Upon this choice depend the issues of life and death.

Fellowship with God fittingly describes life as pictured here. Adam and Eve enjoyed it in the garden of Eden. From that they were sent forth after their fall. The description of Cain, as going "out from the presence of God," shows this fellowship to be unhindered access to his presence.

VIII

Sin

The nature of sin appears as: (1) doubt concerning the truthfulness, love, and righteousness of JHWH God; (2) desire for that which JHWH God has forbidden; (3) disobedience to the command of JHWH God. The first appearance of a word for sin is in Genesis 4:7. It comes from a word meaning to miss the mark or fail. Thus sin is failure to develop into that which God desired us to become.

The author of sin is shown to be a subtle, deceitful, and malicious personality called "the serpent," who is Satan. He is the Bible's explanation as to the entrance of sin into human life. Back of this account, into theoretical questions concerning the possibility of sin, the Bible makes no attempt to go. There is force, therefore, in this story:

An old colored slave, who was also an earnest Christian, often pleaded with his young master to forsake sin. The young master frequently dodged the issue, asking puzzling questions as to how sin got into human life.

One day, he sent the old colored saint to drive some hogs out of a field of fine corn. After being gone for some hours, the old man returned and said, "Master, to sabe my life, I cain't fin' out how dem pigs got inter dat corn."

"Well, did you drive them out?"

"Naw, sir, I'se been tryin' ter fin' out how they got in."

After the master's "cussin" had finally died down, that old man, who knew less about books but more about God and life, said, "Master, it's strange ter me dat you'll spen' all yer time lookin' fer de place where sin got in 'sted er runnin' it out."

This story puts responsibility for sin upon the sinner, upon each and every one who sins. No excuses accepted!

IX

Death

Death is loss of eternal life. Developments of it are hypocrisy in worship, crime, and corruption of every sort. Fundamentally and always it is loss of the life from God.

X

Salvation

Salvation is: (1) victory over the serpent, (2) the work of JHWH, (3) faith in JHWH's promise.

Victory over the serpent is "the bruising" of the serpent's head.

Salvation is of JHWH, because the warfare by the woman and her seed is to be inspired by the prophecy of JHWH as to the final victory.

Salvation is also through faith in the promise of JHWH, inasmuch as JHWH inspires the victory but leaves man to accomplish it.

DETAILED OUTLINE
Theme: Generations of Adam
I

Succession of JHWH worshipers...........5:1-32

II

Corruption of the godly by intermarriage
with the ungodly........................6:1-4

III

Repentance of JHWH that he made man.....6:5-8

TEXTUAL NOTES

The prominence given to names in this section makes us question why these particular ones were selected. Each of the persons was chosen from among many others in his family. The father of each is described as living hundreds of years and begetting sons and daughters. Men indeed multiplied upon the face of the earth, and the naming of these is a real selection.

It hardly seems sufficient to suppose that these were the first-born in their families. If so, the first-born came very late in some instances. Even when so, there may be more to account for the prominence given to the whole group.

There is no emphasis here upon their longevity; it is taken as a matter of course in this passage.

Longevity does distinguish them in our thinking, but that is because the length of earthly existence is pictured afterward as gradually shortening, seemingly because of sin.

When we look at the first three, Adam, Seth, Enosh, we see that they are the three linked with the worship of JHWH by the closing verses of the preceding section. When we look at the end of the list, we find names there very prominent in the promotion of JHWH worship. This leads to the conclusion that all are mentioned because they are worshipers of JHWH.

This leads to another line of study. As the names of those already studied have meanings growing out of their spiritual relations with JHWH, we expect these to have similar meanings. Therefore, we observe the following:

1. Seth (5:6) means Appointed One.

2. Enos (5:9) means Mortal One.

3. Kenan (5:12) may, like Cain, mean Acquired. However, the root came in time to be associated with the work of an artificer, a flute player, or a hymn singer. When we consider the name of his son, we are inclined to consider Flute Player or Hymn Singer as the most likely interpretation.

4. Mahalalel (5:15) means Praise of God.

5. Jared (5:18) means One Going Down or One Prostrating Himself. This name probably refers to a habit of prayer.

6. Enoch (5:21) means Trained One or Dedicated One. The root meant to rub the palate of a newborn child as a midwife did in order to teach it to suck, and later to make experienced or submissive as one trains a horse by a rope in its mouth. The application of these ideas to spiritual discipline is vividly attractive. Doubtless there is close connection between this description of character and the statement, "Enoch walked with God: and he was not; for God took him" (Gen. 5:24). He was the first to be translated from the earth without tasting death, and his experience must have greatly stimulated interest in the blessedness of full fellowship with God beyond the bounds of sinful flesh.

7. Methuselah's (5:25) meaning is very uncertain, but there is a possibility that it is Man Sent or Messenger.

8. Lamech's (5:28) meaning is entirely uncertain.

9. Noah (5:29) means Comfort. The great significance of this and the connection with JHWH worship are brought out at length in the story of the flood.

10. Shem (5:32) means Name. It is entirely possible that he was thus described because his allegiance to JHWH as the Name was outstanding (Cf. notes on Gen. 6:4 and 9:26).

11. Ham (5:32) means Dark.

12. Japheth (5:32) means Fair and likewise refers to color.

6:2. "Sons of God" appears to refer to the JHWH worshipers. The phrase is applied later to God's Chosen People. As we are following here the account of an appointed or chosen line, such use is natural here.

The passage 6:1-4 is one of the most disputed passages in Genesis.

The phrase, "sons of God," is the starting point for divergence of opinions, yet it in itself offers no real difficulties. It appears that all who vary from the interpretation already suggested are controlled here by their interpretation of the problems which follow. There is no ground for the change of "sons of God" to "gods" (Cf. AT) or "angels" (Cf. MNT), unless one thinks "the Nephilim" to be represented as giants, who are offspring of angels and humans and became "men of renown" because of physical prowess. If such interpretation is correct, this passage is truly a remnant of mythology, and it ought to be amended.

Two other types of interpretation for this disputed passage are possible. One would look upon the problem words as words whose meaning has been lost, thereby making a thoroughly satisfactory interpretation impossible. Thus the ASV gives us a mere transliteration in Nephilim, leaving us to guess as to its meaning. The other would seek to interpret these problem words in the light of the context, remembering the list of JHWH worshipers which preceded and the corruption leading to the

Flood which follows, and allowing consistency to be the umpire. We will proceed according to this last method.

"Daughters of men" appears to refer to those not among the JHWH worshipers. Thus intermarriage with them meant intermarriage between the godly and the ungodly.

6:3. "A hundred and twenty years" appears to refer to the period of grace to be allowed before the Flood. The patriarchs after the Flood are credited with much more than one hundred and twenty. How then could a consistent author use this of the life time of individuals?

6:4. "The Nephilim" are the ones referred to at the end of the verse in these words, "the same were the mighty men that were of old, the men of renown." Therefore all these descriptions must stand or fall together.

The part of the verse which is clear is that those described "were in the earth in those days, and also after that"; so we need to start there. "Those days" are the days of intermarriage of the godly with the ungodly and the consequent corruption described in 6:5-8. As "those days" extend to the Flood, the "after that" must refer to the time of the Flood and afterward. Therefore those described appear to be Noah and his sons. They were the only ones who lived both before and after.

If the Nephilim are Noah and his sons, what can Nephilim mean?

The translation "giants" depends solely upon the connection of Nephilim with giants in Numbers 13: 33 and the supposition that "the mighty men" are mighty because of their physical prowess. Numbers 13:33 tells us that the giants described there were "of the Nephilim," descended from Nephilim; but that does not say that the name Nephilim means giants. Numbers 13:33 leaves the meaning of Nephilim an open question. Then, the meaning of "the mighty men" is an open question, and the meaning of the whole passage an open question. Furthermore Noah and his sons are nowhere described as giants. Recognition of that fact evidently led to the use of Nephilim instead of giants in the ASV. At least we have here a situation that cries out for explanation.

"Mighty men" does not necessarily mean men noted for physical might. In Psalm 112:1-2 it is used of sons who inherit the might of him "that feareth Jehovah." Their inheritance is described throughout the psalm as one of spiritual might; graciousness, mercy, and righteousness (Cf. vv. 4-6); trust in JHWH (Cf. vv. 7-8); benevolence and honor (Cf. vv. 9-10). No mention is made of physical might. JHWH himself is compared to such men in Isaiah 42:13.

These mighty men of Genesis 6:4 are also described as "men of the name." This has been changed in our versions to "men of renown." "Men of a name," in Hebrew, means men possessing a reputation or renown; but, "men of the name" can have reference only to the worshipers of JHWH. The only reason for changing the Hebrew text is the conviction that this passage is confused, corrupted, or shows evidence that ideas from later times have been written into it. Is there occasion for such conviction? "Men of the name" agrees perfectly with the context, including "mighty men" when spiritually interpreted. Another fact also lends color to this interpretation. A word for men meaning "mortals" rather than "earthly beings" appears here for the first time. It is the plural of the name Enos (Mortal) in whose time men, recognizing their mortality, began to worship JHWH. It is fitting, therefore, that "men of the name" be pictured as men who recognized their mortal estate and became worshipers of JHWH.

A possible derivation of Nephilim is from the verb meaning to be separate. The only indication of this meaning is in the circumstances of the context and possible parallels in the grammatical development of other great words used to describe spiritual characters from early times like prophets or Nazarites. Nevertheless, the consistency of such a meaning as Separated Ones with the whole of the context is alone sufficient to give strength to this interpretation. The Separated Ones would be that portion of the families of the sons of God which stood apart from intermarriage with the ungodly and consequent corruption.

One further explanation concerning the use of Nephilim in Numbers 13:33 needs to be added. If

Nephilim there is thought of merely as indicating descendants of Noah and his sons, the sentence in which it appears may appear as a truism, unnecessary and incongruous. We need, however, to remember that the meaning of Separated Ones would make Nephilim more of a characterization of JHWH worshipers than a family name. Also by the time of the Exodus some descendants of Noah were still JHWH worshipers, but most of them were not. The memory of their fathers as Separated Ones, men who came out of the division of the nations at Babel (Cf. Gen. 11:1-9) still worshipers of JHWH, might naturally be cherished by the giants at Hebron, yet the fact might not be a matter of common knowledge and its statement a truism.

6:6. "It repented Jehovah" is an anthropopathic expression, one that pictures God as having feelings like those of men. Anthropomorphic expressions, those that picture God as having a physical form like that of man, also occur frequently and are to be interpreted from the same viewpoint. All of them use the language of storytelling to express ideas about God, describing him in terms of the being that is most like God, but not intending to attribute to him the limitations of mankind. Thus, God's hand describes his power touching earthly affairs but not a physical hand. Such language is common to the language of all men and is easily understood. Even so, the repentance of God is not to be thought of as implying limitations upon the wisdom of the original plan and unforeseen necessity of alteration of the plan, as man's repentance would imply. Repentance here is equivalent to the qualifying words which follow, "grieved him at his heart."

THEOLOGICAL STUDIES
XI
Worship

True worship is shown to be: (1) trust in JHWH; (2) praise, prayer, and discipline in the name of JHWH; (3) separation from the sins of the world.

DETAILED OUTLINE
Theme: Generations of Noah
I

Noah's walk with God......................6:9-12

II

Preservation of the race from
    destruction........................6:13 to 8:19

III

Making another covenant............8:20 to 9:19

IV

Prophecies concerning the blessings
    of JHWH worship....................9:20-29

TEXTUAL NOTES

6:9. "Perfect" means sound or having integrity, not sinless. It is synonomous here with righteousness (Cf. Gen. 7:1). Also it is qualified by "in his generations (times)," so as to indicate that he is perfect according to the standards of his time (Cf. Gen. 7:1).

The second "generations" of this verse is an entirely different word from the first, the one used to head the ten divisions of the book. The root idea of the second is a circle. It may be applied to a circle of dwellings, a cycle of time, or the people living in that cycle of time. This "generations" indicates a cross-section of time or society without linking the persons included by ties of blood or influence. The other "generations" does indicate ties of blood and influence, there being a causal connection in all cases.

6:12. "Earth," the equivalent of "all flesh," applies to life on the earth. The corruption of the earth was so universal as to threaten even the chosen ones. The purpose of the Flood appears to have been to preserve and magnify their influence as well as punish the corrupt ones.

6:13; 7:1. The variation of the name of God appears to need no more explanation generally than a desire on the author's part for variation. Yet oftentimes, as here, a deeper reason is probable. Those parts of the story which speak of God's personal and exclusive relation with his worshipers use JHWH, others God. (Cf. 8:20-22 with 9:1-17). In other words, the intimate, personal, and peculiarly precious experiences of men's spiritual salvation were wrapped around the name JHWH.

7:2. The added command about clean beasts looked to the continuation of worship, as seen in 8:20. It was not a contradiction of the command in 6:19, but an addition to it.

8:21. "Jehovah smelled the sweet savor" is another anthropopathic expression. It simply indicates the pleasure of JHWH, because of the worship of this family upon whose influence he depended for propagation of his worship in the world.

9:3. The use of animals was extended to include meat for food.

9:5. The higher value of human life is emphasized.

9:6. The value of man's life is made the basis for capital punishment. The necessity, in general, for the sacrifice of one who is a killer to save the lives of many is assumed.

9:20-27. The purpose of this story seems to be the presentation of the prophecies at the close. The Bible never avoids or whitewashes the sins of God's people. At the same time it never gives accounts of sin without a goodly purpose. The shame and condemnation of sin are portrayed so as to show that it is the grace of God and that alone that saves men from their sins.

9:22. "The father of Canaan" is added here to the name of Ham to show that the curse upon

Canaan was a result of the influence of his father.
Ham showed no sense of shame because of his
father's sin. His telling of his brothers was doubtless the work of a laughing, mocking tattletale. This
is evidence of an attitude toward sin that is bound
to breed mischief and ruin, most probably in the
lives of one's own children, who are most apt to be
seductively influenced by it.

9:23. The actions of Shem and Japheth manifest
shame, desire to protect, and hope of helping.

9:24. Noah's understanding manifests insight
which leads to the following prophecies as to what
the consequences of the attitudes of his sons will be.
Shame and repentance on Noah's part also are implied.

9:25. The curse does not condemn individuals
regardless of their attitude toward God. This is
shown by the experience of Melchizedek in Abraham's day, Rahab in Joshua's time, and the Syro-
phenician woman whose urgent prayer won a blessing from Jesus. All these were Canaanites.

The curse does prophesy that Ham's attitude will
influence Canaan—probably the influence was already evident to Noah's experienced eyes—and Canaan's descendants so as to enslave and subjugate
a race through lasciviousness.

9:26. The mention of JHWH as "the God of
Shem" shows that Shem's high standards of moral
conduct were derived from the worship of JHWH,
also that Shem was a leader in that worship. The

possibility that the name Shem (Name) was given because of his allegiance to the worship of "the Name" is emphasized by these facts.

9:27. "Dwell in the tents of Shem" probably means share the blessings of Shem, especially the blessings of the worship he championed.

ARCHEOLOGICAL SIDELIGHTS

I

Primitive Traditions

Parallel Reading: Price, Ira M., *MOT*, chap. VII (Compare the Genesis stories with the primitive, nonbiblical traditions); Muir, James C., *HTE*, pp. 9-21; Yahuda, A. S., *Accuracy of the Bible*, pp. 131-207; Mallowan, M. E. L., "New Light on Ancient Ur" in *National Geographic Magazine;* Vol. LVII, No. one, January 1930.

THEOLOGICAL STUDIES

XII

Effects of Sin

The effects of sin are shown to be: (1) universal, (2) damning, (3) subject to effective resistance only by faith in JHWH.

The universality of sin appears in the corruption of the human race before the Flood and the persistence of sin even among those saved from the Flood.

The damning effect of sin appears in God's repentance that he made man and the curse upon

Canaan. The God who strove so faithfully to save mankind, Cainites and Canaanites included, would have saved all if he could. Having made man able to sin, even God is unable to save those who refuse his salvation from the damning effects of sin. That is what grieves him "at his heart."

Only those who do respond to God by faith can effectively resist sin.

DETAILED OUTLINE

Theme: Generations of the Sons of Noah

Introduction

Historical note..............................10:1

I

Settlers of the isles and coastlands..........10:2-5

II

Settlers of Babylonia, Assyria, and Canaan..10:6-20

III

The Hebrews (children of Eber).........10:21-32

IV

Division of the nations at Babel............11:1-9

TEXTUAL NOTES

A series of expressions running through the account of each group of peoples shows that the chief center of interest in the account is the division of the nations at Babel, and that the causes for the division are of special significance to the message of Genesis. This series of expressions is as follows:

10:5. Of these were the isles of the nations divided in their lands.

10:11. Out of that land (Babel) he went forth.

10:14. Whence went forth the Philistines.

10:18. Afterward were the families of the Canaanite spread abroad.

10:25. The name of the one was Peleg; for in his day was the earth divided.

10:32. Of these were the nations divided (Cf. 11:4, 8-9).

The causes of this great division are given in 11:4. There we note:

1. The purpose to build "a city." Archeology shows that the cities of that time were city states, centers of kingdoms.

2. The purpose to build "a tower." The description, "whose top may reach unto heaven," most probably meant very high. Doubtless it also had a religious significance. "The Tower of Babel or Babylon . . . was a structure peculiar to Babylonia and Assyria. According to all accounts, and judging from erections extant in those countries, Babylonian towers were always rectangular, built in stages and provided with an inclined ascent continued along

each side to the top. As religious ceremonies were performed thereon, they were generally surmounted by a chapel in which sacred objects or images were kept."[9] The religious significance of this tower, planned to "reach unto heaven," was that its heathen god was considered the supreme power in heaven and earth, and the kingdom built around his worship was intended to dominate the earth.

Associated with the religious ceremonies at such a tower or *ziggurat,* as it was called in Babylonia, were priests and priestesses who were devoted to prostitution in the name of religion. Thus such a tower stood for the vile moral degradation to which idolatry had led. Yet the men of Babylon wanted to make this kind of abomination the center of a world state.

3. The purpose to "make us a name." The three purposes appear vitally connected, so that the worship at the tower was to gain for the people a name which would permanently unite all peoples in a kingdom. The idea was a seed-form of the world-wide kingdom which characterized the Babylon of later history. Moreover, it had in it the fatal purpose "to make us a name," the purpose of self-exaltation, which makes all man-made plans for a world-wide kingdom to be directly opposed to the kingdom of God. To put "a name for us" at the center of religion and the state is to set up humanity in the place of the Name, JHWH.

[9]Pinches, T. G., "Tower of Babel," *ISBE.*

When we observe the point of these purposes, we understand that the division at Babel was a momentous spiritual experience in the lives of JHWH worshipers as well as an historical explanation of the dispersion of the nations. Their descendants cherished the memory of the loyalty of these forefathers in the faith, who went forth seeking freedom for their faith. It is not necessary to suppose that all or any great number of those who went forth went solely for the sake of their faith. Widespread division provokes purposes of all sorts. But, conflict between the worship of JHWH and the deification of power was the fundamental cause of the dispersion, and those in the line of promise cherished the memory of those men whose loyalty to JHWH was outstanding at this time. Therefore, prominence was given to Shem and Eber (Cf. 10:21) and providential frustration of Babel's purpose by JHWH (Cf. 11:5-7).

11:9. Babylon, in the language of the Babylonians, meant "Gate of God." So they intended it! The Bible uses the idea of confusion, taken from a similar word, to describe it. Probably this play on words was intended as a means of mocking the purposes of its founders, saying that such purposes are doomed by JHWH himself to accomplish the very opposite of what the authors intend.

Generations of Shem 11:10-26
TEXTUAL NOTES

A portion of the generations of Shem was given in the preceding section, but only that part leading to the division of the nations, because that was the center of interest there. Now the whole is given, because the connection with Terah, the father of Abraham, is the objective.

11:14. Eber means Crossing Over. The name may describe Eber as one who emigrated. Certainly it marks him as the father of the Hebrews. Gen. 10:21 takes care to point out that Shem was the father of all the children of Eber, the Hebrews, thereby emphasizing the relations of Shem, Eber, and the Hebrews. When Moses and Aaron explained to Pharaoh who JHWH was, they called him, "The God of the Hebrews" (Ex. 5:1-3). Thus Shem, Eber, and the Hebrews are lined up as followers of JHWH.

All this tells us why the whole line of Shem means so much as a tie with Terah and Abraham.

ARCHEOLOGICAL SIDELIGHTS
II
Division of the Nations

Parallel Reading: Price, Ira M., *MOT*, chapter VIII (Locate as many nations as possible on a map. Compare biblical and nonbiblical references); Adams, J. McKee, BB, pp. 25-35; Yahuda, A. S., *Accuracy of the Bible*, pp. 208-214; Pinches, T. G., "Babel, Babylon," in ISBE, vol. I, pp. 350-358.

DETAILED OUTLINE
Theme: Generations of Terah
Introduction

Movement of Terah and his family toward
Canaan 11:27-32

I
Promises to Abraham

1. Promise of a homeland...................12:1
2. Promise of a great nation as his posterity.12:2a
3. Promise of a blessing upon him and all who
   bless him 12:2b-3
Con. Canaan pointed out as the Promised
   Land 12:4-9

II
Rescue from Egypt

Providential protection and return to the
   Promised Land 12:10-20

III
Separation from Lot

1. Prosperity and renewal of worship.......13:1-4
2. Abram maintains peace by giving Lot his
   choice of the land....................13:5-13
3. JHWH assures Abram that all the Promised
   Land will be for him and his seed......13:14-18

IV
Rescue of Lot

1. Abram rescues Lot from Eastern invaders
   along with the spoil of Sodom and
   Gomorrah 14:1-16
2. Righteous disposal of the spoil........14:17-24
   a. Dedication of a part to God
      Most High by giving a tithe
      to Melchizedek 14:17-20

    b. Rejection of any spoil for
        himself 14:21-24
3. Assurance of protection and of a child of
    his own as an heir....................15:1-21

V
Birth of Ishmael

1. Sarai and Abram plan for an heir by
    Hagar 16:1-16
2. JHWH plans for an heir by Sarai, changing
    the names of both accordingly.........17:1-27

VI
Intercession for Sodom and Gomorrah

1. The plan of JHWH to destroy leads
    Abraham to pray for the sparing of the
    righteous 18:1-33
2. Sodom and Gomorrah destroyed, but Lot
    and his descendants blessed for Abraham's
    sake................................19:1-38

VII
Providential protection in Gerar

1. Abraham again rescued from results of
    falsehoods concerning Sarah 20:1-7
2. Abraham's conduct overruled so as to make
    him a blessing to Abimelech............20:8-18

VIII
Birth of Isaac

1. Sarah's concern for Isaac presses Abra-
    ham to send away Hagar and Ishmael...21:1-11

2. God approves the separation, yet blesses
   Ishmael and his descendants for
   Abraham's sake 21:12-21

IX
Covenant with Abimelech

Peace with the Philistines and a covenant
to do kindness each to the other is established
because Abimelech saw that God was with
Abraham 21:22-34

X
Offering of Isaac

1. Abraham's complete trust in JHWH
   proved 22:1-14
2. JHWH swears to make the faith of
   Abraham a blessing to all nations......22:15-19
(Historical notes) 22:20-24

XI
Death and Burial of Sarah

Patient faith, waiting till the hour of
necessity, and nobility of character, making
his neighbors recognize him as "a prince of
God," lead to a willing grant of Abraham's
request to purchase a possession in the
Promised Land 23:1-20

XII
Finding a Wife for Isaac

By keen practical wisdom on one hand,
seeking a wife from among JHWH wor-

shipers (Cf. 24:3, 37) and guarding at the
same time against temptation to forsake the
Land of Promise (Cf. 24:6); and by providence of JHWH and his angel (Cf. 24:7, 11-
15, 40-49) on the other; provision is made
for the continuance of the promised seed...24:1-67
(Historical notes concerning marriage to
Keturah, death and burial)...............25:1-11

TEXTUAL NOTES

12:6. "And the Canaanite was then in the land"
is looked upon by some as a remark that must have
been unnecessary at any time before the Canaanites
were dispossessed by the Israelites, and therefore as
evidence of late authorship. It needs to be noted
that Abram was approaching the moment when
JHWH said, "Unto thy seed will I give this land"
(12:7). Knowledge of Noah's prophecy concerning
the Canaanites was very probably brought to mind
by his sojourn in their land. In any case, it is fitting
for any account of his experience to recall the fact
that the Canaanite was there, so as to indicate that
he received the promise by faith alone.

12:7. "An altar to Jehovah" shows that Abram
brought with him a knowledge of JHWH, also that
the name JHWH was linked with the promises to
Abram from the beginning.

12:8. "An altar to Jehovah" shows that it became a habit with Abram to set up his family altar
wherever he stopped in the Promised Land.

12:13. "My sister" expressed a half-truth (Cf. Gen. 20:12). However, the impression conveyed— and it was the impression intended to be conveyed —was a whole lie. There is no effort here to cover the fact that Abram sinned. The point of the teaching is that God saved him from the consequences (12:17-19) and restored him to the Land of Promise (12:20).

13:4. "Unto the place of the altar" tells of renewed worship in the land. There is no account of an altar in Egypt.

13:18. "An altar unto Jehovah" adds a chapter in this story of Abram's worship.

14:14. "As far as Dan" is another expression which appears to many to reflect the work of an author later than Moses. The Dan referred to here is in northern Palestine; and, so far as records show, it was not known as Dan till the tribe of Dan left its appointed inheritance and settled there (Cf. Judges 17-18). Even if so, this description of the place would appear to be merely an explanation intended to help those of a later time understand the story. It would in no sense vitiate the teaching of the original or prove anything as to the authorship of the original.

14:18. "Melchizedek" means My King is Righteousness. The teaching about Melchizedek, as a type of the eternal priesthood of Christ (Heb. 7), does not signify that he was born without father or mother, but that his appearance in this passage is without mention of father or mother. Thus that which is chance appearance in his case is taken as an example of what is literally true concerning the eternal Christ.

"Salem" means Peace. It is generally considered the same city as Jerusalem, City of Peace.

"God Most High" was evidently accepted by Abram as describing the same God as his God. The description, "possessor of heaven and earth," in 14:19, accords with the story of the Beginning and suggests that "God Most High" meant first of all Creator (Cf. Deut. 32:8 and many passages in Daniel, beginning at Daniel 3:26). God Most High was evidently the name for the true God among Gentiles. These facts account for the recognition accorded Melchizedek by Abram in giving to him a tithe of the spoil he had taken.

15:1. "Fear not" shows that Abram feared reprisals from the Eastern invaders. They were kings with armies that ravaged far and wide; he merely the head of a small band, so far as human aid was concerned. But, JHWH said to him, "I am thy shield." Just so, the rescue of Lot and consequent fear were merely occasions in the life of Abram for renewed and enlarged assurances concerning those things JHWH had promised him.

15:2. "Lord Jehovah" is used here for the first time.

"Lord" is a title meaning Master or Ruler. In its ordinary form it is used of men as well as God

(Cf. 23:6). Here, however, we have a plural with the pronoun my attached. This form is used of God alone. It is the title substituted for JHWH in later usage. The use of the whole expression as a distinctive title for God appears oftentimes to render the idea of the possessive pronoun entirely unnecessary; yet the whole expression is retained as a title expressing intimate acquaintance and ardent loyalty, being the exact equivalent of the English word Lord when used of God.

The combination of Lord with JHWH is the most significant fact here. Certainly Abram did not use the title as the equivalent of the Name, for if so he need not have used both. Why then did he add the title to the Name? The Name appeared previously as a description of the personal character of God; the immanent God who reveals himself to men and deals with them in love, truth, and righteousness; in a word, the God of the covenants. "Lord," according to this context, describes the office or position of God; the transcendent, sovereign God who rules the uinverse and controls the events in the life of his people; in a word, the master of providence. The use of the two together reflects a conviction on Abram's part that the Lord's sovereign control of events in his life will be fulfilled according to the covenant promises of JHWH. Together they give a surpassingly rich and practical view of God.

15:18. "Made a covenant" is literally "cut a covenant." The idea of cutting is associated with the sacrifices, "divided in the midst" (15:10), between whose pieces passed "a smoking furnace and a flaming torch" (15:17). These sacrifices were blood sacrifices, doubtless symbolizing the sacredness which a "blood covenant" has had among all peoples of all times. Different opinions as to details may be studied in Shultz's *Old Testament Theology*, Vol. II, p. 3f. and in Fairbairn's *Typology of Scripture*, Vol. I, p. 305f. However, they certainly emphasize the assurance given to Abram concerning the Promised Seed, including the sojourn and bondage (15:13), preparatory to an exodus (15:14), and possession of the Promised Land (15:18).

16:7. "The angel of Jehovah" appears here for the first time. It is significant that he is *the* angel. There is none other like him. When he spoke (16:10), he assumed authority over the giving of life as JHWH himself. Moreover, Hagar said of him, "Thou art a God that seeth," and the author identified him with JHWH (16:13). These facts fill us with wonder as to the relation of the angel of JHWH to JHWH, even as Hagar's experience filled her with wonder, but no further light is thrown upon the problem here.

17:1. "God Almighty" or *"El Shaddai"* (ASV footnote) is interpreted in various ways. *El* is a short form of Elohim, and its meaning is clear, but the meaning of *Shaddai* is doubtful. The rabbis of old thought it meant the One Who Is Sufficient. Some students today derive it from a verb meaning to deal violently; some form a noun meaning a woman's breast. All these meanings point in the same general direction, and the conclusion of Davidson fits the situation very well, "The phrase El Shaddai may be simply an intensification of El itself . . ."[10] We may add that it is thus an intensification of Lord also, and emphasized one side of that great combination Lord JHWH. As such it fits in a peculiar sense the assurance of chapter 17 concerning the ability of JHWH to give Abram a child in his old age.

17:5. Abram means Exalted Father. Abraham means Father of a Multitude. The new name was a token of the promise, and Abram's acceptance of it a token of faith in the promise concerning the seed.

17:15. Sarai probably means Contentious (Cf. 16:6). Sarah means Princess. As Sarai passed from contentious striving over the problem of an heir to regal assurance of fulfilment of the promise through her, even in her old age, she became Sarah.

17:19. Isaac, meaning Laughter, was a most fitting name for this child, the promise of whose coming could produce the incredulous laughter of doubt (Cf. 18:12-15), and whose actual coming would produce hilarious delight in fulfilment of the seemingly impossible (Cf. 21:5-7).

17:22-27. Circumcision became the symbol, sign, or token (Cf. 17:11) of the Abrahamic covenant, for Abraham and all his descendants. As it was not given till after the making of the covenant of chapter fifteen, Abram's faith and salvation are shown as not dependent upon it. On the other hand, as

[10]Davidson, A. B., *TOT*, p. 42.

other symbols of covenants with God, it promotes fulfilment of the terms of the covenant.

18:17-19. These verses show that the chief point of the stories in this group is not the fate of Sodom and Gomorrah but the spiritual development of Abraham. This accounts for the inclusion of the story of the visit to Abraham preceding that of the visit to Sodom. Likewise in each group of stories, the spiritual development of Abraham is the theme that binds all together.

18:20-21. Here again God's feelings and thoughts are described as being like those of men. We observed previously that such description must not be construed as teaching that God is limited as man is. This passage does not teach that it was necessary for God to go down to Sodom in order to perceive the facts about men of Sodom. However, it does teach a deep truth which we easily overlook. We need to take care lest our efforts to avoid the first error cause us to make another and miss the true teaching.

Here JHWH tells Abraham what he intends to do to Sodom, so that he may bring out the righteousness and justice of Abraham and fulfil thereby "that which he hath spoken of him" (18-19). Also he goes down to Sodom to prove in men's eyes the moral vileness of Sodom and bring thereby upon Sodom the punishment he knows already to be her desert. JHWH does not act upon his omniscience and foreknowledge alone in his condemnation of sinners or salvation of believers. He enters into their lives in

such ways as to let their own choices and actions
prove them to be what he knows they are.

19:30-38. In this black picture of Lot's descendants we have another illustration of the fact that
it is the spiritual influence of Abraham that is the
theme of all these stories. As said in 19:29, "God
remembered Abraham, and sent Lot out of the midst
of the overthrow." That he did despite Lot's sin.
Accordingly, despite the sordid facts concerning their
birth, the blessing of Abraham's influence continues
upon Lot's descendants, as later history testifies.

20:7. "Prophet" occurs here for the first time.
The word means One Made to Bubble Over. Second
Peter 2:5 calls Noah "a preacher of righteousness,"
which amounts to the same thing. Jude, verse 14,
says that Enoch prophesied. Abraham, however, is
the first named as a prophet by the Old Testament.
All these men were spokesmen for God and this
seems to be the import of the word "prophet."

21:33. "Everlasting God" or "God of the Ages"
is another description of the character of JHWH.
The covenant with Abimelech flooded the feeling
of Abraham with conviction that the blessings of
JHWH upon him and through him would flow on
forever, and he used this new name to express the
conviction that the ages are under the control of
JHWH.

22:14. *"Jehovah-jireh"* or "Jehovah will see and
provide" (Cf. ASV footnote) is explained by 22:8.
It expresses complete faith in the providence of
JHWH.

ARCHEOLOGICAL SIDELIGHTS

III

Reflection of Babylonian Life in the Stories of Abraham

Parallel Reading: Price, Ira M., *MOT*, sections 99-106, 113-117 (Does archeology today tend to discredit or confirm the stories of Abraham?); Adams, J. McKee, *BB*, pp. 36-81; Muir, James C., *HTE*, pp. 21-47; Woolley, Leonard, *Abraham*.

THEOLOGICAL STUDIES

XIII

Promises to Abraham

The promises to Abraham, viewed in the light of his full experience, reveal a deep significance in their purpose, their requirements, and their provisions.

1. Purpose. In a word, the purpose is the provocation of faith.

Like the first promise, the First Evangel in the garden of Eden, these promises precede any corresponding human experience. They precede the covenants which follow and provoke the response which makes mutual agreements possible. They proceed purely out of the heart and purpose of JHWH. They tell us that JHWH takes the initiative in salvation, and that they are means of grace whereby he provokes faith.

2. Requirements. As means of testing faith, the promises require the giving up of native country,

kindred according to the flesh, and worldly birth-right.

3. Provisions. As means of developing faith, the promises provide for a gift from God corresponding to each sacrifice, a promised land, a promised seed, and a promised blessing.

The promises vitally affect all sacred history that has followed and all interpretations of that which is yet to come. If we would understand the Bible, we must understand these promises.

All three promises are vitally linked to one another. The land is essential to the development of the seed. The land and the seed are essential to the development of the blessing.

The blessing is pregnant with spiritual teaching. Its descriptions show that it includes:

1. Union with God. God first says, "I will bless thee"; later, "Be thou a blessing." The imperative at the last calls for confirmation of the will of God by the will of Abraham. Thus it must ever be with those who receive the blessing of JHWH God.

2. Greatness of character. A name in the Bible regularly stands for character rather than mere reputation.

3. Universal influence upon destiny. All who respond favorably to the work of God in him and his seed are destined to be blessed. All who respond unfavorably to the work of God in him and his seed

are destined to be cursed. This corresponds to Jesus' description of the influence of the church in Matthew 16:16-19.

XIV

Faith of Abraham

The experiences of Abraham likewise cast a flood of light upon the origin and nature of faith. They reveal the justification of Paul's description of Abraham as "Father of believers" (Gal. 3:6-9, 29).

1. Origin.

Faith appears as a free and active movement of will. Even as the promises provided for a response corresponding to the purpose of JHWH, so it developed in every story. The outline shows how each one of the twelve stories leads to a spiritual struggle and a victory of faith. The promises constantly challenge him; Providence protects him and corrects him; and in every story faith arises and claims a promise. Stories I-III portray his struggle to grasp the promise of the land. Stories IV and V portray his struggle to grasp the promise of the seed. Stories VI-X portray his struggle to grasp the promise of the blessing. The last two portray his confident claim of all the promises. Upon one promise after another faith climbed to the sublime height reached in the offering of Isaac. All Abraham's experiences are characterized by the explanation given in Genesis 15:6, "And he believed in Jehovah; and he reckoned it to him for righteousness."

There is no contradiction between this teaching and Ephesians 2:8, which says, "By grace have ye been saved through faith; and that not of yourselves, it is the gift of God." The word for gift does not agree in gender with the word for faith, so could not refer to it. The verse teaches that the plan of salvation is of God but not the faith in the plan, and so do the experiences of Abraham.

There is truth in these words of "The Water Lily" which fits the experience of Abraham:

> O star on the breast of the river!
> O marvel of bloom and grace!
> Did you fall right down from Heaven
> Out of the sweetest place?
> You are white as the thoughts of an angel,
> Your heart is steeped in the sun;
> Did you grow in the Golden City,
> My pure and radiant one?
>
> Nay, nay, I fell not out of Heaven;
> None gave me my saintly white;
> It slowly grew from the darkness,
> Down in the dreary night,
> From the ooze of the silent river
> I won my glory and grace.
> White souls fall not, O my poet,
> They rise—to the sweetest place.

At the same time faith appears as a response to the promises and providences and character of God.

The water lily must rise, but at the same time it rises in response to the light of the sun. The water lily had to have a bulb with a living seed therein, but the sun made its bed and brought the season that awoke that seed. The water lily had to sprout and grow and bloom; but the sun sent the light that warmed its heart, drew its tiny, tender growth upward out of the night, brought it into the light of day and the glory of a flower. So the faith of Abraham was drawn by the light of JHWH.

2. Meaning. The following points inhere in the nature of Abraham's experiences:

(1) Trust. A feeling of confidence in JHWH develops steadily into complete reliance upon him.

(2) Belief. Intelligent recognition of many articles of faith are manifested. Among them the following are prominent:

The love, truth, and righteousness of JHWH are recognized, when the promises are believed; and that belief is reckoned for righteousness. The reckoning was not merely done by JHWH, but also recognized by Abraham.

The name Lord JHWH recognizes that JHWH rules everything in accord with the moral principles of his love, truth, and righteousness.

El Shaddai, God Everlasting, and *JHWH-Jireh* intensify and apply the meaning of Lord. *El Shaddai* signifies that the power of the Lord JHWH not merely may overrule but wills to overrule the laws of nature in order to provide for fulfilment of the promises, as in the birth of Isaac. God Everlasting signifies that this providential rule of the Lord

JHWH will determine the course of the ages. *JHWH-Jireh* signifies that the Lord JHWH will utilize this providential control, so as to develop the faith of his children, doing whatever is necessary to produce that faith and make it a blessing to all peoples.

Appearance of JHWH to the physical senses of man is identified with the angel of JHWH. The angel is God's representative in the fulfilment of his promises and covenants.

(3) Hearkening to the voice of JHWH. This description of the climax of faith is given in Genesis 22:18, describing the willingness of Abraham to sacrifice Isaac. "Obeyed my voice" is literally "hearkened to my voice." It does not describe the act of obedience, as may be observed from the distinction between "obey my voice" (hearken to my voice) and "keep my covenant" in Exodus 19:5. It describes that faith which is the counterpart of the act of obedience, inseparable from it, identified with it. This identification accounts for the variations in translation of this idea.

XV

Covenant with Abraham

The promises of JHWH and the faith of Abraham are united in the making of the Abrahamic covenant. We note, therefore, the following points concerning the nature of this covenant:

1. It is conditional. The condition of faith is quite obvious in Abraham's experiences. Likewise in all the experiences of his seed this condition of faith must apply. Complete fulfilment of the promise concerning the blessing cannot come apart from faith in JHWH on the part of the seed.

2. It is certain. The spiritual blessings of JHWH are never unconditional; but, for the faithful, they are certain. Genesis 18:19 is an outstanding statement of this great truth. The children of Abraham according to the flesh are adopted of JHWH (Cf. Rom. 9:1-5). They are adopted because Abraham's faith under the providence of God is able to propagate itself among them. Their adoption is absolutely fixed and sure, because JHWH swears to accomplish it (Cf. Gen. 22:16-18; Rom. 9:6-12; 11:25-32). Yet this adoption is not arbitrary or unrighteous, for it is to be accomplished according to the moral principles of the character of JHWH, by the wooing of the seed unto acceptance of the same salvation by faith that Abraham enjoyed and Paul preached (Cf. Rom. 9:14 to 11:24).

3. It is universal. Because its conditions are moral and spiritual, yet its fulfilment certain, this covenant is a means of universal blessing. The development of its fulfilment is to furnish illustrations of the salvation by which JHWH will save all who will exercise faith in him. There is no restriction but rather a demonstration of the grace of God, the purpose of which is to save as many as possible as quickly as possible.

TEXTUAL NOTES
Generations of Ishmael

25:12-18. The brevity of the generations of Ishmael is striking. All developments other than those that further the explanation of the salvation of JHWH are quickly dismissed. This account furnishes some historical connections, but that is about all. We remember, therefore, that Ishmael "abode over against all his brethren" (25:18).

DETAILED OUTLINE
Theme: Generations of Isaac
I
Esau and Jacob

1. Birth of twins in answer to prayer, with prophecy of Jacob's ascendency........25:19-26
2. Esau despises his birthright...........25:27-34

II
Inheritance of the Blessing of Abraham

1. The promises renewed upon the condition that he remain in the Promised Land.....26:1-5
2. Providential protection overcomes opposition and makes Isaac's influence a blessing to his neighbors 26:6-35

III
Blessing of Jacob

1. Contrary to the intentions of Isaac..27:1 to 28:5
(Historical note concerning Esau's wives)...28:6-9
2. Assured by JHWH ....28:10 to 35:15
   (1) JHWH brings Jacob into a covenant at Bethel.........28:10-22

  (2) JHWH prospers him in
      Paddan-aram ....29:1 to 30:43

  (3) JHWH brings him back to the
      Land of Promise ....31:1 to 32:2

  (4) JHWH brings him into peace
      with Esau ....32:3 to 33:17

  (5) JHWH protects him from the
      consequences of the sin of
      Simeon and Levi .....33:18 to 35:15

(Historical notes concerning the birth of
  Benjamin, death of Rachel, and so forth) 35:16-29

TEXTUAL NOTES

25:21. Isaac was a man of prayer and trust in JHWH.

25:22. Rebekah was also one who trusted in JHWH.

25:23. This is prophecy indicating election "according to the foreknowledge of God" (1 Peter 1:2), but not mechanical and unrighteous fixing of future events (Cf. Rom. 9:10-14).

25:25. Esau means Hairy One.

25:26. Jacob means Supplanter.

25:27-28. The partiality of Isaac and Rebekah is the root of much of the trouble that follows, and is thus the provocation for chastisements from JHWH that are also prominent in their lives and that of Jacob.

25:31. The birthright included a double portion of inherited property and leadership of the tribe in judgment, war, and worship. Leadership in worship in this case involves "the blessing of Abraham," as Isaac called it in Genesis 28:4. This included the promises to Abraham. The promises made this feature peculiar to JHWH worshipers. As already seen, these promises are not to be fulfilled arbitrarily, but according to the moral principles of JHWH. The awarding was therefore not necessarily to the first-born, as was usual with others. The awarding of this birthright depends upon the faith of the recipient. The awarding of it is the theme of all the stories about the generations of Isaac, and furnishes supremely important and discriminating illustrations as to how the blessings of JHWH are bestowed.

Esau's attitude toward the birthright and toward the blessing revealed his lack of spiritual understanding. In Genesis 27:36 he is revealed as thinking that he might receive the blessing, though he had lost the birthright. While the birthright, as a mere double portion of possessions, and the leadership, in the sense of rule, could be divided between servants of JHWH like Judah and Joseph (Cf. Gen. 48:3-6; 1 Chron. 5:2), it was not possible among JHWH worshipers for either to go to a spiritually blind person like Esau. There could be a material blessing for him, such as Isaac finally predicted, but not one of these tokens of JHWH's special favor.

Jacob's offer to purchase the birthright reveals failure on his part to appreciate fully the moral nature of the blessing of Abraham. Certainly it could not be bought and sold! One redeeming fact, however, is revealed by his offer. He valued that blessing. His desire for it was a basis for appeal, instruction, and correction.

25:34. The fact that "Esau despised his birthright" is the point of the story. That which he did was indicative of his character. There was nothing in him to appeal to, to instruct, and to develop into an inheritance of the blessing. In God's sight the birthright was never his, and the sale of it was a "Comedy of Errors." The birthright was his only according to a natural expectation of men, but not according to the moral judgment of JHWH.

26:1-5. The obedient loyalty of Isaac to JHWH stands out here. Jehovah was "the Fear of Isaac," as Jacob testified. Accordingly he inherited the blessing of Abraham.

26:6-11. Nevertheless, Isaac was susceptible to the same temptations as his father and was saved by the same kind of providences. The recurrence of such sin is in no sense strange when we observe the habits of men.

26:12-22. Isaac gave up many so-called rights for the sake of peace with his neighbors. The victory of peace at Rehoboth was his reward. Also with peace came prosperity.

26:23-33. The covenant at Beersheba was a spiritual triumph like that of Abraham at the same place. It gives an added reason for calling the place Beersheba. That does not make either experience a copy of the other, as some have charged. The similarity in the names of the kings described may be accounted for by the use of inherited titles. The meaning of Abimelech, The King is My Father, suggests that. The parallel between Abraham's and Isaac's godly influence upon Abimelech, like that of their lying, is not an occasion for wonder. Similar characters in similar circumstances naturally have similar experiences. At the same time there are differences in Isaac's story which indicate that his experience was real. The description of Abimelech as hating Isaac before this time is a prominent fact, and it makes the triumph of Isaac an ever greater spiritual victory than that of his father.

Chapters 27-35. The inclusion of these chapters among the generations of Isaac makes us wonder as to the reason, because they appear at first glance to deal almost exclusively with Jacob. The theme of this section, the inheritance of the blessing of Abraham, furnishes the explanation. The second heir, Jacob, is tremendously affected both by the virtues and faults of Isaac. All of those influences are used of God in transforming Jacob, the Supplanter, into Israel, God's Prince. Those influences, despite conflicts and contradictions, are overruled by JHWH so as to bring forth this transformation. Such is the wonder of the work of God!

27:1-40. The overruling of Isaac's intention to give the chief blessing to Esau made Isaac to recognize the purpose of JHWH to give the blessing of Abraham to Jacob. This in turn gave hope to Jacob that sustained him as he was sent away to Paddan-aram. That hope must have been burning in his heart as he left home, as he lay under the stars at Bethel. That hope prepared him for what God said to him at Bethel.

Nevertheless, there were many things wrong with the contentions of Isaac's family over the birth-right. Esau was not the only one who was wrong. Isaac was spiritually shortsighted in his judgment of his sons; he did not ask JHWH for guidance in the matter; he was selfish and dotingly fond of a worldly son. Rebekah and Jacob used trickery and deceit.

Moreover, the multiplying of wrong never makes right. The good that came out of this struggle was not accomplished by the deceit of Rebekah and Jacob, but by the chastisements of JHWH. Isaac, who should have ruled with wisdom and unselfish-ness, was overruled; Rebekah lost the companionship of her darling boy, never to see him again on earth; Jacob was forced to face many long years of hard-ship away from father and mother; and yet by these chastisements JHWH made all things work together for good. It was absolutely necessary for JHWH to chastise in order to save his children.

28:10-22. The vision and promises drew from Jacob a response that brought him into covenant relations with JHWH. We may not be able to say when Jacob was converted, but he certainly gave evidence here that he was converted either then and there or previously. There he entered into covenant relations and experienced the spiritual equivalent of "joining the church."

29:1 to 30:43. The hard dealing and deceit of Laban constituted a school of hard knocks for Jacob. To come out of the quiet life he enjoyed under his mother's favoritism and father's inactivity (Cf. Gen. 25:27-28) into this school was an important part of the making of Jacob. He came out of this school attributing his prosperity to God (Cf. Gen. 31:6-13).

31:1 to 32:2. JHWH told Jacob to return (Cf. 31:3). JHWH protected him from Laban (Cf. 31:42). Thus God gave him assurance of constant protection, which was a great preparation for the supreme test that lay ahead (Cf. 32:1-2).

32:3 to 33:17. The climax of Jacob's development came at Peniel.

The prospective meeting with Esau was the great test that led to this development. The possibility of vengeance, provoked by his own wrongdoing, had to be faced. His messenger brought word that Esau was coming with a company of four hundred men. Four hundred men with him could mean nothing less than a band of desert raiders, such as Bedouin chieftains led in the slaughter and spoil of lonely caravans.

Jacob's first preparation included plans for the use of gifts and shrewdness (Cf. 32:8). There was prayer and assurance (Cf. 32:9-12). Nevertheless, a good deal of dependence upon wealth and self was still in him (Cf. 32:13-21).

The complete and only sufficient preparation came at Peniel. He put his family across the brook Jabbok while he turned back. Rachel, his beloved, and little Joseph were last. Furthest from danger! He had done all his wealth and shrewdness could do up to the actual meeting. Yet he turned back. Not because he was a coward! Not because he would fail to be in front when the meeting time came! His preparation was not complete. With a heart nigh to breaking, because he knew he needed a higher power more than ever before, he turned back—alone —to seek God.

The wrestling that took place there at Peniel was the wrestling of prayer. The "man" that wrestled with him was the angel of JHWH, as Hosea 12:3-4 tells us. Jacob realized that fact before he was through, for he called the place Peniel, The Face of God. His identification of the angel with God is seen again in Genesis 48:15-16. The failure of the angel to prevail was not lack of physical power, for soon he touched Jacob's thigh so as to cripple him for life. The failure was failure to bring him to that point of spiritual development which is surrender and victory at the same time. This development was assured by crippling him. The suggestion of the angel that he might go was not for his sake but for the sake of the effect on Jacob. Then Jacob was led to lay hold upon him with the only claim whereby a man can prevail with God—prayer.

The experience at Peniel was the climax of the transformation that shuffled off the old sheath of Jacob, the Supplanter, and revealed the new man, Israel, the Prince of God. Israel primarily means Wrestler with God. Its root refers to physical wrestling. But it comes to be used of a prince as one who wrestles mentally and spiritually in councils of state with his sovereign.

After Peniel, Jacob went on easily and gloriously to a peaceful understanding with Esau. That peace, however, was assured by JHWH. As for Jacob, he limped his way into this victory; and his chastisement stands till this day as a memorial to remind all the children of Israel of the price of successful spiritual striving with God and with men (Cf. 32:31-32).

33:18 to 35:15. Providence and chastisement went on and on with Israel. He suffered both inwardly and outwardly from the sins of his sons at Shechem (Cf. 34:30). He needed indeed to get back to Bethel, and revive his spiritual experience. Without providential protection (Cf. 35:5), he might not have lived to do so, but he did (Cf. 35:9-15).

CRITICAL PROBLEMS
V
Parallel Stories

Study the parallel of Genesis 20:1-18 and Genesis 26:6-11, also that of Genesis 21:22-34 and Genesis

26:26-33. Compare the following: 21:31 with 26:33, 28:18-19 with 35:14-15, 32:29 with 35:10.

In connection with these matters, H. E. Ryle says, "So far as the composite character of the literary structure of Genesis is concerned, the main conclusions of criticism may be said to be established."[11] To what conclusion does he refer? What do you think about these conclusions?

ARCHEOLOGICAL SIDELIGHTS
IV
Reflection of Syrian and Assyrian Life in Stories of Jacob

Parallel Reading: Price, Ira M., *MOT,* section 118 (Do archeological findings affect the story of Jacob?); Muir, James C., *HTE,* pp. 47-49.

THEOLOGICAL STUDIES
XVI
Chastisement

The chastening experiences of Isaac and Jacob abundantly illustrate the teaching of Hebrews 12:5-15. They show that the chastening of God is:

1. Essential (Cf. Heb. 12:5-8). Jacob was made an heir to the blessing of Abraham by chastisement rather than by purchase of the birthright or a deceitfully sought, unwillingly uttered blessing.

2. Profitable (Cf. Heb. 12:9-10). The contentious wrongs of Isaac, Rebekah, and Jacob were destructive; but, under chastening Providence, they

[11]Ryle. H. E., "Genesis," *HDB,* p. 143.

were overruled so as to provoke spiritual profit, partaking of holiness, which is santification.

3. Peaceable (Cf. Heb. 12:11-13). Gradually Isaac, Rebekah, and Jacob were brought into a peace which was the highest joy of all. The contrast in the case of Esau is pathetic. He failed to bring any abiding satisfaction to his parents, despite his efforts to please them by marrying a daughter of Ishmael.

XVII

Election

Election receives a classic illustration in the case of Esau and Jacob (Cf. Rom. 9:10-13). In Jacob's case it is election unto salvation, but in Esau's it is election unto condemnation.

1. Election unto salvation. Jacob's experience fulfils the teaching of 1 Peter 1:2 in each of the following steps:

(1) "According to the foreknowledge of God, the Father." The word to Rebekah concerning the destiny of her children was a prophecy. Like the First Evangel, like the Promises to Abraham, this was to Rebekah and Jacob a provocation of faith. It may be that without such provocation their desire to believe would have failed in the face of the misunderstanding of Isaac and the suffering caused by their own wrongdoing; and so God gave it in order to assure that right and truth would prevail in the end.

(2) "In santification of the Spirit."

The crux of the whole matter was Jacob's desire for the blessing of Abraham. That expressed a love of spiritual things. It expressed faith in JHWH. The Spirit could lead a soul like that through all the experiences of sanctification.

Assurance of the fulfilment of faith went on in Jacob's life as it does in the lives of other saved persons. We are led to the conclusion that all saved persons are elected of God. The lack of announcement does not affect the election one way or another. The announcement in Jacob's case appears to come because of his mother's and his special need. Certainly it did not remove the necessity for the exercise of personal faith and the development of that faith under the chastening providence of God.

(3) "Unto obedience and sprinkling of the blood of Jesus Christ." Obedience resulted from faith on Jacob's part and providence on God's part, according to the moral principles of JHWH. The completion of God's providence came in the atonement of Jesus Christ and availed for Jacob as for any other believer before or after its historical accomplishment.

2. Election unto condemnation. Esau's experience was the exact opposite of Jacob's.

(1) According to the foreknowledge of God.

The announcement to his mother was according to the foreknowledge of God—in this case, however, a foreknowledge of doom. It too was a prophecy of what would come to pass. However, it certainly must have come to pass whether prophesied or not. God is never represented in the Bible as doing anything that would make him responsible for the loss of any soul.

(2) In spite of the leading of the Spirit.

When Esau despised his birthright he did despite to the Spirit. He manifested a complete lack of spiritual appreciation. When he tried later to make a distinction between the birthright and the blessing, when begging his father to bless him despite the blessing already given to Jacob (Cf. Gen. 27:36), he manifested spiritual blindness. He speaks of the birthright with the leadership it conferred as something separate from the blessing. Evidently the blessing to him was merely freedom to do as he pleased, combined with prosperity. But such could not be among the people of JHWH. The whole point is that he completely lacked spiritual understanding of JHWH, had no faith in JHWH, and for that he was condemned. So it is with all who are condemned.

(3) Unto disobedience and rejection of the atonement of JHWH. Through physical prowess, natural leadership, and a generosity that could be prodigal in its lavishment while lacking in spiritual purpose, Esau became chieftain of Edom; yet he remained a "profane person" (Cf. Heb. 12:16). Even the atonement of JHWH God and the Lord Jesus Christ cannot touch him.

Generations of Esau

36:1-43. Historical connections are chief points of interest here. The names of Eliphaz and Teman (36:4, 11) may be associated with Eliphaz, the Temanite, of the book of Job. The name of Uz (36:28) helps us to locate Job himself (Cf. Job 1:1).

DETAILED OUTLINE

Theme: Generations of Jacob

I

Strife Among His Sons

1. Jacob's love for Joseph makes his brothers hate him 37:1-4
2. Joseph's dreams make his brothers envy him 37:5-11
3. Consequently Joseph is sold into slavery in Egypt 37:12-36
(Historical record concerning Judah)......38:1-30

II

Preservation of All Israel in Egypt

1. Joseph's righteousness causes him to be thrown into prison....................39:1-23
2. Joseph's faithfulness in prison leads to interpretation of dreams for Pharaoh's butler and baker 40:1-23
3. Joseph's favor to Pharaoh's butler leads to interpretation of a dream for Pharaoh.41:1-36
4. Joseph's interpretation leads to his appointment as Premier of Egypt........41:37-57

5. Joseph's rule of Egypt is used to preserve
the life of his people.............42:1 to 47:26
   (1) His brothers are forced by
   famine to come to him.........42:1-6
   (2) Joseph, unknown to his brothers, tests them...........42:7 to 44:34
   (3) Joseph explains and fulfils the
   providence of God in bringing
   all of them to Egypt.....45:1 to 47:26

III

Assurance of Blessing for All Israel in the Land of Promise

1. Jacob makes Joseph swear to bury him
in the Land of Promise...............47:27-31
2. Jacob blesses his children.......48:1 to 49:33
3. Joseph fulfils his oath.................50:1-14
4. Joseph assures his brethren...........50:15-26
   (1) Of their preservation.........50:15-21
   (2) Of their return.............50:22-26

TEXTUAL NOTES

37:2. The prominence of Joseph is noticeable from the very beginning of this section.

37:5, 9. These dreams were received as revelations by Joseph, and that fact was evidently a chief source of spiritual strength through all that followed. The assurance of ultimate success was a refuge when he suffered. The assurance that all these things, the things that make suffering and success, were of God was a faith that glorified his whole life.

37:25-28. Midianites were also Ishmaelites. This fact is pointd out in Judges 8:22-24.

37:35. Sheol is here referred to for the first time. It is indicated as the place of departed spirits, for Jacob thought Joseph to be dead and said, "I will go down to Sheol to my son mourning."

38:1-30. The importance of Judah comes into view here. There are important historical connections shown by the relation of Perez, Judah's son, to the lineage of David and Jesus (Cf. Ruth 4:12, 18; Neh. 11:4-6: Matt. 1:3; Luke 3:33). The contrast of Judah's life at this time with that revealed in his plea for Benjamin in Genesis 44:18-34 adds to the mere historical facts a vision of a man with a changed heart. This explains why Judah was to become so important. Not his sins but his change makes this extended story of his sins worth while.

39:1 to 47:26. Through all these stories runs a chain of providences that lead to the preservation of Israel in Egypt. The dominating purpose of the author to make this obvious appears at every turn.

Along with the major emphasis run two other important developments which are magnified later. One is that of Joseph, the other of Judah. Both suffered for the sake of their brethren, and they became both servants and leaders thereby. Joseph's interpretation of his own suffering is given in Gene-

sis 45:4-8. It shows his suffering to be a part of
God's plan to preserve Israel along with a host of
others, and it reveals a nobility of character in him
that is glorious.

The great development of Judah is brought to a
climax in Genesis 44:18-34. This description of his
plea for Benjamin by Dr. John R. Sampey is most
fitting:

> When Joseph's stratagem puts Benja-
> min in his power, Judah pleads the cause of
> his youngest brother, and nobly volunteers
> to abide in his stead as a slave of Joseph.
> Judah's speech on behalf of Benjamin is
> the most pathetic in all literature. He, too,
> like Joseph, is brought face to face with the
> doctrine of the cross; and he hesitates not,
> but bravely offers himself as a substitute
> for his guilty brother. Inasmuch as Judah
> anticipated the substitutionary sacrifice
> of the Christ, it was fitting that he should
> be placed at the head of his brethren as
> ruler. From Judah should spring the
> Prince of Peace, unto whom the peoples
> shall be obedient (Gen. 49:8-12).[12]

47:27 to 51:26. Every experience here looks
toward the return to the Land of Promise. The burial
of Jacob there, the solemn preparation of Joseph to
have his bones carried back, and everything associated with these matters looks toward the fulfilment

[12]Sampey, John R., *The Heart of the Old Testament*, p. 41.

of the promises. So it is with Jews around the world until this day in their desire to be buried in the Holy Land.

Accordingly, Jacob's prophecies concerning his sons in 49:2-27 look toward the fulfilment of the promises in every case. Keen spiritual discernment of their characters is matched with discriminating distinctions as to their destinies, and these are very instructive.

Reuben is deprived of his birthright because of grievous sin. "The pre-eminence of dignity, and the pre-eminence of power" are identified with "my might and the beginning of my strength." All these referred, not to Reuben's character, but to the dignity and power brought to Jacob by the birth of his first-born son. That was blighted by Reuben's sin. Therefore, he was deposed from his place. We need to observe, however, that he was not deprived of a place among his brethren, only of the leadership. That fact in itself was a prediction of a change and a limited influence for good.

Simeon and Levi are likewise condemned to suffer for their sins, particularly their vengeance upon the men of Shechem. Their anger is cursed; yet, they are allowed places among their brethren, "In Israel" but scattered. Fulfilment of this is found in the wandering of Simeonites from the allotted inheritance south of Judah, so that in later history they no longer appear as a separate tribe. Yet Simeon continues to be counted as one of the twelve.

More blessed influences come to Levites, particularly through Moses and Aaron, but the effect of this early evil influence is observable at many points in their history. Ezekiel 44:11 reflects both sides.

Judah is given the place of leader. His natural strength is pictured in the phrase, "as a lion." Ability for leadership, when once chastened and consecrated as his did come to be in his offer to suffer in Benjamin's stead, is one of the main pillars of the kingdom of God. His rule over his brethren is described as culminating in the coming of Shiloh. The prophecy adds finally, "Unto him shall the obedience of all the peoples be," indicating a universal kingdom.

"Until Shiloh Come"

The meaning of the phrase, "Until Shiloh come," has been interpreted in many ways. David L. Cooper argues convincingly for this interpretation, "until he come" whose it is:

> The well known passage of Ezekiel 21:27 undoubtedly is an echo of these words, if we accept the Septuagint translation as a faithful reflection of the original. The prophet's statement is . . . . . . "until he come whose right it is." Ezekiel's referring to this one in so familiar and so brief a manner without any explanation proves that he assumed, on the part of his audience, a general knowledge and common expectation of the coming of this great Autocrat . . . . . . It is undoubtedly an echo of

Jacob's prediction, since there is no other passage to which it can point.[13]

All can see that this interpretation makes the phrase refer to the Messiah. It is therefore well to remember that Jacob indicated that the fulfilment of these things belongs "in the latter days."

If we question as to how Jacob was led to make this messianic prophecy, we must remember the word of hope in the First Evangel about a promised seed. That promise must have been associated by JHWH worshipers with those in the line of promise, Seth, Noah, Shem, Eber, Abraham, Isaac, Jacob, and Judah, as he is now being given the pre-eminence.

This prophecy is an expression which makes an exceedingly important advance over all previous expressions concerning the promised seed. Probably this hope had been taking shape gradually in the hearts of those who were assured that they belonged to the line of promise, yet who knew deep down in their hearts that a greater than they must come before their victory over self and the serpent could be complete. This prophecy appears to speak of a coming one whose character was already perceived by those within the circle of the elect. This coming one is thus reflected as an ideal and universal ruler to arise out of the tribe of Judah.

Zebulun is to dwell by the sea, and Issachar to be "under taskwork." Reasons for the assignment

---

[13]Cooper, David L., *Messiah: His Nature and Person*, p. 48.

of Zebulun are not given, but we may be sure that a natural bent of his own character played an important part, even as in the case of Issachar. In the case of Issachar this natural bent appears in the words "a strong ass" and "he bowed his shoulder to bear." Always the will of the individual plays a major role in the making of destiny. Environment plays one. God's grace plays the supreme one, where there is the right response. Will, however, is never deposed, only inspired and aided by the grace of God.

Dan's treacherous nature is not spared. Power to "judge his people" is indicated, but lack of all benevolent spirit is significant. The stories in Judges 8, illustrate his influence. Verse 18 may have been intended as an ominous warning to Dan, indicating that Jacob had been saved from sinister impulses by waiting for the salvation of JHWH, but that as yet there was no evidence of such trust in Dan.

Gad, Asher, and Naphtali are each given some word of praise and hope, but there is nothing of special importance beyond their places among the twelve.

Joseph is promised fruitfulness and spiritual blessing in an unbounded degree, yet not in a way irreconcilable with the dominance of Judah.

The prophesied fruitfulness applies to multiplied posterity and is fulfilled in the size of the tribes of Ephraim and Manasseh. "The blessings of thy father" appear to apply chiefly to this same point, when we observe that Jacob's previous description of those blessings to Joseph (48:3-4) stressed chiefly the increase of his own posterity. In expectation of the fulfilment, Jacob had already taken Ephraim and Manasseh as his own sons and directed that each inherit as his other sons. This amounted to the same thing as giving a double portion to Joseph. Even so the tribes of Ephraim and Manasseh did each receive a portion when the Promised Land was divided by Joshua.

The spiritual blessings are described as coming through his suffering and special help from God. "The arms of his hands were made strong, by the hands of the Mighty One of Jacob." When Jacob added, "From thence is the shepherd, the stone of Israel," he probably referred to the angel of JHWH. He had previously identified the angel with God in describing the blessings that had come to his own life (48:15-16). Thus he makes us see the angel watching over Joseph throughout his days, making the dishonesty of his brothers to develop his own honesty (37:2), making the wantonness of Potiphar's wife to develop his purity (39:7-18), making the cruelty of his brothers to develop his own kindness (45:4-7), making the fearful dependence of the defenseless to magnify his magnanimity (50:15-21). Joseph combined purity, tenderness, forgiveness, ambition, business ability, statesmanship, and faith in God in a spiritual nobility that must prevail "unto the utmost bound of the everlasting hills."

Two such careers of leadership as these prophesied for the tribes of Judah and Joseph are bound to clash and destroy each other unless the rule of Judah and the influence of Joseph can be reconciled. Jacob predicted universal extent for both. The problem of the reconciliation evidently dawned upon Jacob even as it does upon us. His consideration discerned the hope of all as taking shape thus: (1) the spiritual royalty of Joseph's character in vicarious suffering; (2) the strength of Judah in loving, saving, messianic power.

Benjamin's picture is by no means good. The stories of Judges 19:1 to 21:25 tell of the terrible consequences. When the impulses of a beast of prey are observed in one's nature, that ought to be a fearful warning. It carries threats to every sacred privilege of unborn generations. It is almost a wonder that Benjamin was left a place in Israel.

CRITICAL PROBLEMS

VI

Unity of Genesis

Parallel Reading: Moller, Wilhelm, "Genesis" in *ISBE*; Ryle, H. E. "Genesis" in *HDB*; Driver, S. R., "Genesis" in *LOT*.

Suggested questions and parallel concerning subsidiary matters:

1. Are the patriarchs "personifications" or individual historical characters?

Orr, James, *POT*, pp. 88-98; Ryle, H. E., "Genesis," in *HDB*, p. 147; Moller, Wilhelm, "Genesis," in *ISBE*, p. 1212; Woolley, Leonard, "The Authority of the Tradition" and "The Written Testimony" in *Abraham;* Marston, Charles, "Primeval Religion and the Ten Patriarchs" in *The Bible Is True*.

What kind of unity is there in the stories of Genesis? The product of a great editor, who reconciles his material, or a compilation with conflicting teachings?

Orr, James, *POT*, pp. 27-38, 53-64; Driver, S. R., *LOT*, pp. 4-20; Moller, Wilhelm, "Genesis" in *ISBE*, pp. 1200-1205; Ryle, H. E., "Genesis" in *HDB*, pp. 143-147; Green, Wm. H., *Unity of the Book of Genesis;* Delitszch, Franz, *NCG;* Skinner, John, "Genesis" in *ICC*.

ARCHEOLOGICAL SIDELIGHTS

V

Reflection of Egyptian Life in the Joseph Stories

Parallel Reading: Price, Ira M., *MOT*, Sections 119-122; Yahuda, A. S., "The Joseph Narrative," in *The Accuracy of the Bible;* Marston, Charles, "The Coming of the Shepherd Kings," in *The Bible Is True;* Adams, J. McKee, *BB*, pp. 104-110; Muir, James C., "Israel in Egypt," in *HTE;* Orr, James, *POT*, pp. 111-116, 413-417.

THEOLOGICAL STUDIES

XVIII

Vicarious Suffering

Vicarious suffering is shown to be:

1. A means of preserving the lives of others (Cf. 45:5).

2. A means of most blessed influence upon the spiritual betterment of others. Joseph's submission to the will of God in this way made him an instrument for the provocation of Judah's plea for Benjamin. The love, sagacity, and magnanimity of each in this way continues to bless them and others.

3. A means of glorifying those who willingly yield themselves as channels of its blessings. As Judah and Joseph subjected themselves by self-sacrifice for others' sake, they were freed thereby to be the best that was in them and the best that God had for them.

4. A high means of accomplishing the providence of God (45:7, 8).

XIX

Messiah

The character of Messiah, though the title is not coined till quite late in Old Testament times (Cf. Dan. 9:25-26), takes shape as:

1. The angel of JHWH, Jacob's identification of the angel with JHWH in Genesis 48:15-16, reveals his recognition of this wonderful being as the immediate representative of JHWH in his dealing with his people, bringing immediate, easily grasped assurance of the salvation of JHWH to the physical senses of the elect.

2. The savior of Israel. Jacob's references to "my glory" in Genesis 49:6, and "the shepherd, the stone of Israel," in Genesis 49:24 picture the angel as a spiritual savior.

"My glory" was appealed to for the perservation of Simeon and Levi from the evil influence of their natures on each other; in other words, "their assembly." Divided, scattered, they are seen as inheriting places in Israel; but the divine influence of the angel is seen as necessary to keep them apart, so as to prevent the stirring up of their fierce anger and preserve the good that is in them. This appeal shows that "my glory" must needs be interpreted as a personality, one of such character as to bring a curse upon their anger while leaving to them a hope of salvation.

"The shepherd, the stone of Israel" is likewise pointed out as the one who is from, more exactly of, "the Mighty One of Jacob." The salvation of Joseph, accomplished by this one, is identified with the work of the hands of "the God of thy father . . . the Almighty."

3. The rightful judge of Israel: (1) to whom judgment belongs (Cf. Gen. 49:10 and Ezek. 21:27); (2) who is to come of the tribe of Judah (Cf. 49:10 and Micah 5:2); (3) who is to come in the latter days (Cf. 49:10 and Isa. 2:2-4, Micah 4:1-5).

4. The eventual sovereign of a universal kingdom (Cf. Gen. 49:10 and Isa. 11:10).

INTRODUCTION TO EXODUS

Parallel Reading

Moller, Wilhelm, "Exodus, The Book of," *ISBE*

Harford-Battersby, G., "Exodus, The Book of," *HDB*

Conant, Thomas J., "Exodus," *SBD*

Driver, S. R., "Exodus," *LOT*

Name and Theme

The Jewish name of Exodus is composed of its first two words. Their translation is, "And these are the Names."

The name Exodus means "a going out" and refers to the departure of Israel from Egypt. It has come from the Septuagint, through the Vulgate, to our versions, and bears no relation to the Jewish name.

The theme is not touched by either of the names for the book; they are purely accidental or popular. Even ours does not take into account the latter part of the book or the real purpose of its message. The theme is the making of the covenant with Israel. This covenant is made with Israel as a nation and involves broader matters than those covered by the covenants with Abraham, Isaac, and Jacob.

Date and Authorship

Date and authorship are a part of the question as to date and authorship of the Pentateuch, and they will be left for final consideration until we have examined all of the Pentateuch.

Plan and Purpose

The covenant idea will be found to prevail through all sections of the book. In the latter half it is obvious. In the first half, preparation for it is apparent as soon as we study the meaning of the experiences recounted. The deliverer is one prepared to tell suffering Israelites that JHWH is ready to fulfil his promises to Abraham, Isaac, and Jacob; in other words he is a prophet of the covenant obligations of JHWH. At every turn in the story of deliverance, JHWH reminds Israel that he is fulfiling his promises, must fulfil his promises, and will fulfil them; in other words, he is a covenant keeping God. All is a preparation for the making of a covenant with the nation.

GENERAL OUTLINE OF EXODUS

Theme: Covenant With the Nation of Israel

A. Oppression of the covenant people in
    Egypt 1:1-22

B. Preparation of a deliverer...........2:1 to 7:7

C. Deliverance ....7:8 to 18:27

D. Making of the covenant..........19:1 to 24:18

E. Plans for the covenant symbols...25:1 to 31:18

F. Breaking and renewal of the
    covenant ....32:1 to 34:35

G. Institution of the covenant
    symbols ....35:1 to 40:38

DETAILED OUTLINES

Theme: Oppression of the Covenant People in Egypt

I. Rapid increase of Israel in Egypt........1:1-7

II. Reduction of Israel to slavery........1:8-14

III. Killing of the boy babies............1:15-22

Theme: Preparation of a Deliverer

I

Preservation of Moses

1. Providential nurture, adoption, and
   education 2:1-10
2. Futile attempts to help his people......2:11-15
3. Exile in Midian 2:16-22

II

Call

1. Occasion: God's knowledge of Israel's
   suffering 2:23-25
2. Purpose: deliverance of Israel from Egypt.3:1-10
3. Debate ....3:11 to 4:17
   (1) Concerning Moses' fitness......3:11-12
   (2) Concerning Moses' knowledge
       of God 3:13-22
   (3) Concerning the response of the
       people 4:1-9
   (4) Concerning handicaps in de-
       livery 4:10-12
   (5) Concerning unwillingness 4:13-17

III

Discouragement

1. Return to Egypt 4:18-31

2. Release of Israel demanded in the Name...5:1-3

3. Pharaoh increases the burdens of Israel...5:4-14

4. The people blame their troubles on Moses
   and Aaron 5:15-21

5. Moses questions the power of the Name to
   save ....5:22 to 6:1

IV

Assurance

Int. Faithfulness of JHWH to his covenant
   stressed 6:2-5

1. Promise to relieve Israel 6:6a

2. Promise to free Israel....................6:6b

3. Promise to redeem Israel.................6:6c

4. Promise to adopt Israel.................6:7a

5. Promise to be Israel's God................6:7b

6. Promise to bring Israel into the Promised
   Land 6:8a

7. Promise to give the Promised Land as a
   heritage 6:8b

Con. Israel fails, because of hardships, to
   have faith in JHWH......................6:9

V

Charge

Int. Occasion: the fainting faith of Moses. .6:10-13
(Historical identification of Moses and
    Aaron) 6:14-27
1. To see that the call of JHWH is endow-
    ment with power ....6:28 to 7:1
2. To speak all that JHWH commands........7:2
3. To make Egyptians know the power of
    JHWH 7:3-5
Con. Obedience of Moses and Aaron.........7:6-7

TEXTUAL NOTES

1:7. The increase of Israel is described in four different ways in order to stress its abundance. In one way that increase was a blessing. In another it was the occasion for the troubles that followed.

2:1. "A daughter of Levi" is identified in 6:20 as Jochebed. Her name means JHWH Is Glorious. The use of JHWH in her name is evidence of the cherished nature of the Name among the Israelites. Maybe not many of them cherished it as Jochebed and her family. However, the worship of JHWH was alive, and the effects were glorious.

2:9. The nurture of this child by his mother was a blessed providence. In the school at mother's knee the love of JHWH was planted. Other schools might increase his understanding of JHWH worship and ability to apply it to world affairs, but none could supersede that school at mother's knee, for there the love of JHWH was planted.

2:10. "And he became her son" tells us that he was given the best education of the schools of Egypt, the education of an Egyptian prince.

Stephen said, "And Moses was instructed in all the wisdom of the Egyptians; and he was mighty in his words and works."[1] Evidently Stephen thought that the wisdom of the Egyptians had made an important contribution to the mighty words and works of Moses.

The schooling of a young prince was much like that of the Prince of Wales in modern times. He was given experience in all phases of his people's life. He was not expected to be a luxurious despot, not in ancient Egypt. Thus Moses learned the economic structure upon which one of the greatest civilizations of early history was built, as well as other secrets of her wisdom.

However, the learning and riches of Egypt were devoted to idolatry. They were lavished upon temples and tombs which symbolized the worship of a multitude of idols. The living of the people, even the best of it as expressed in their temples, was lascivious to a shocking degree, prostituted by the ideas of idolatry. Their hopes for eternity, as expressed in their tombs, were hopes for blessings as grossly material as the things they enjoyed here and as grossly immoral. Thus pictures of heaven included harems. This was the life upon which Moses

---
[1]Acts 7:22.

turned his back. This was the life which continued to lure the Israelites with its seductiveness when they made the Golden Calf.

The author of Hebrews said, "By faith Moses, when he was grown up, refused to be called the son of Pharaoh's daughter; choosing rather to share ill treatment with the people of God, than to enjoy the pleasures of sin for a season; accounting the reproaches of Christ greater riches than the treasures of Egypt."[2] Evidently the author of Hebrews thought that Moses saw in the treasures of Egypt a temptation to enjoy the pleasures of sin.

When considering the wisdom of Egypt or any worldly culture from a biblical viewpoint, the recognition of these two sides becomes important. We observe them in every phase of Egyptian civilization. The fundamental necessity of the early training in JHWH worship is therefore apparent.

2:11-15. Here Moses cast his lot with his own people, choosing the side of JHWH. Nevertheless, his first efforts to help were unguided and futile. The results made his experiences a school of hard knocks, which the Lord overruled so as to bring out good as he did for Jacob.

2:16-23. The school of the desert received Moses next. There courtesy won a home. The years taught him patience. His relatives doubtless added to the store of knowledge which is utilized in Genesis.

---

[2]Hebrews 11:24 to 26a.

The open spaces taught nature study. His profession as a shepherd prepared him to shepherd Israel in the wilderness.

All the other schools led Moses into the highest of all, the school of personal experience with God. We see, in what follows, its doors thrown open for us to observe and also to learn.

2:23-35. We are told here that God "took knowledge" of the situation in Egypt. The call of Moses that follows is the response of JHWH to that situation.

3:1. "Moses" is placed emphatically. This emphasis becomes significant when we observe that the author of Exodus has not emphasized anything up to this point. In 1:1 to 2:25 there are a few emphases in quotations, such as speakers naturally and usually employ in conversation, but in the words of the author not a single one. This was evidently planned so as to throw the floodlight on Moses at a dramatic moment.

"Mountain of God," arouses our interest to a higher pitch. This description of a mountain prepares us to look for a revelation.

3:2. "The angel of Jehovah" fits such a scene of revelation.

"A burning bush" completes the scene. It is highly dramatic of course, calculated to arrest Moses' attention and ours too. Doubtless that is exactly why such a means of revelation was used.

Moreover, its symbolism should burn the point of the revelation into every quickened spirit. He who reveals himself in the burning bush burns like a fire but is never consumed. It was not with him as Israel under Egypt's cruel load thought of him, as Moses after forty years of wilderness wandering and loneliness had probably begun to conclude. He could not forget and be unfaithful to his covenant. He is the Faithful One.

3:6. The identification of the angel with "the God of Abraham . . . Isaac . . . and Jacob" bears out what we have observed in Genesis.

3:7-9. The purpose of JHWH to deliver is stated very positively. No doubt is left that JHWH will deliver Israel and do it at this time.

3:10. Yet JHWH desired to work through Moses. The will of JHWH and the call of his servant are two sides of the same thing. The two will become identified in the work of JHWH. JHWH is in his servant, and his servant in JHWH.

3:11 to 4:17. When Moses said, "Who am I?" he was thinking of the man against whom charges of manslaughter and treason had been docketed in Egypt forty years before, also the man who tried to help his brethren and failed. His past rises like a specter that haunts his present and future. But! —God's answer was this simple word, "Certainly I will be with thee."

"I Am That I Am"

The original word for "I will be" is the same word translated immediately afterward, in 3:14, "I Am." As this word is emphasized by repetition in the statement, "I Am that I Am," and then identified with JHWH, it becomes exceedingly important. Therefore it is exceedingly unfortunate that the connection between these three uses of the word and the Name has been obscured in our versions. A footnote in the ASV shows that this word can be translated "I will be" as well as "I Am"; yet most of us overlook the significance of that note. That note should make us realize that either the "I Am That I Am" or "I Will Be That I Will Be" is merely a repetition of the assurance given by "I will be with thee." God assures Moses that what he has said he will be he will be. He is the Faithful One who keeps every promise. This attribute of faithfulness is identified with JHWH and is a very important step in the making of the Name to be a synonym for the moral attributes of God.

The idea of the Eternal, which is often used in interpretation of this passage, arises from this attribute of faithfulness. It expresses faithfulness unlimited as to time or quality. However, this idea of the Eternal is an abstract one which seems out of place in this vivid scene, amid its very practical and simple lessons.

The faithfulness of JHWH is an answer for every excuse Moses had to offer. When he looked at his past, JHWH reminded him that he would be with him. When he foresaw the people's question, "What is his name?" he knew they would be testing his knowledge of God, asking him to tell his experience with God so as to prove his knowledge of God. JHWH showed him that the reminder just given furnished an experience to relate and a vision of an attribute of God which is a basis for the trust of all men. The people's response and his handicaps in delivery are real problems, but they can be met by the same assurance. The fundamental cause of all excuses, unwillingness, is likewise met. When JHWH says, "I will be with thee," there is no room left for excuses.

This new interpretation of JHWH thus emerges as the objective of the story of the Burning Bush. The artistic resources of storytelling are taxed to bring forth this jewel of spiritual teaching in a setting fitted to attract the admiration of every child of God. We discover, moreover, as we carefully examine this setting, that the name JHWH was entirely omitted from the first two chapters even as were the author's emphases. Accordingly we conclude that he used his art from the beginning of Exodus until this point to bring forth this interpretation as a crown jewel of his faith.

This method of identifying JHWH with God corresponds exactly to the arrangement in the early chapters of Genesis. It hints strongly that the same skilled hand shaped both accounts.

4:24-26. The experience in the inn on the way to Egypt may be interpreted as an illness of Moses overruled of JHWH so as to correct a serious defect in his conformity to the ritual and remove an unnecessary hindrance to his influence in the approaching struggle. When "Jehovah met him and sought to kill him," the illness seemed to human eyes to express a desire on God's part for his death. In that case Zipporah, thinking the reason why God should allow such a threat to come to him to be their failure to circumcise their son, proceeds to remedy the neglect. To have gone to the Jews with an uncircumcised son would have been to despise the symbol of the Abrahamic covenant. Thus Zipporah seems to have considered the neglect an act which brought bloodguiltiness to her husband, making him deserve the threat to his life. The remedy was accepted, "so he [JHWH] let him alone." In other words, JHWH allowed him to recover.

5:1 to 6:1. The first results of the appeal to Pharaoh were certainly discouraging in the extreme. Then Moses found himself in a typical preacher's predicament. The Lord was behind him, Pharaoh on one side, the people on the other, and the only way out was to go forward by faith and faith alone. At first his faith began to faint. However, he carried his discouragement to the Lord rather than letting it drive him away from the Lord.

6:2-9. The calm answer in this most tantalizing hour was, "I am Jehovah." The sovereign certainty of that calm assurance is majestically serene and supremely inspiring to the soul of the prophet.

6:10 to 7:7. The charge proceeds upon the expectation that the assurance of JHWH will be appropriated. "And Moses and Aaron did so," in 7:6, tells us that it was appropriated. Thus the Name became their power.

CRITICAL PROBLEMS

VII

The Meaning of Exodus 6:2

The statement, "By my name Jehovah I was not known to them," is interpreted by those who accept the documentary theories concerning the authorship of Exodus as being a contradiction of passages which put JHWH in the mouths of the patriarchs. The following are examples of opinion:

Driver, S. R., "Commentary on Exodus" in *CB*, p. 42; Eiselen, F. C., *Books of the Pentateuch*, p. 128; Fosdick, H. E., *A Guide to Understanding the Bible*, p. 1.

Those of conservative tendencies touching these documentary theories see possibilities of reconciling these Scriptures. Examples on this side are:

Davidson, A. B., *TOT*, p. 68; Oehler, Gustav F., *OTT*, p. 98, note 5; Green, Wm. H., *Higher Criticism of the Pentateuch*, p. 100; Orr, James, *POT*, p. 225.

In weighing this problem, the student should bear in mind the fact that the verb "to know" is distinguished in Hebrew from the verb "to be acquainted with." Instances in which knowledge, as described by this verb, is certainly distinguished from acquaintance; i.e., lack of knowledge is asserted while acquaintance obviously exists, are found in Judges 16:9, Psalm 9:20, Ezekiel 20:9. This distinction is maintained in modern Hebrew. When we observe that Exodus 6:2-8 very carefully explains that a revelation of the name is being given at this time that exceeds in meaning what has been grasped beforehand, this distinction is seen to also apply here. Thus occasion for thinking the passage contradicts Genesis entirely disappears.

ARCHEOLOGICAL SIDELIGHTS

VI

Pithom and Raamses

Parallel Reading: Price, Ira M., *MOT*, section 123; Muir, James C., *HTE*, pp. 59-65; Marston, Charles, "Life of Moses" in *The Bible Is True.*

DETAILED OUTLINE

Theme: Deliverance of Israel

I

Plagues on The Egyptians Win Recognition of JHWH as God

Int. Warning wonders are displayed.........7:8-13
"Pharaoh's heart was hardened [strong]" (7:13).

1. Water turned to blood................7:14-25
   JHWH said, "In this thou shalt know
   that I am Jehovah" (7:17)
   "And Pharaoh's heart was hardened
   [strong]" (7:22).

2. Frogs 8:1-15
   Moses said, "That thou mayest know
   that there is none like unto Jehovah
   our God" (8:10).
   "Pharaoh . . . hardened [made heavy]
   his heart" (8:15).

3. Lice 8:16-19
   "Then the magicians said unto Pharaoh,
   This is the finger of God." (8:19a).
   "And Pharaoh's heart was hardened
   [strong]" (8:19b).

4. Flies 8:20-32
   JHWH said, "To the end that thou
   mayest know that I am Jehovah in the
   midst of the earth" (8:22).
   "And Pharaoh hardened [made heavy]
   his heart this time also" (8:32)

5. Murrain 9:1-7
   Moses said, "And Jehovah shall make a
   distinction" (9:4).
   "But the heart of Pharaoh was stubborn [heavy] (9:7).

6. Boils 9:8-12
   "And the magicians could not stand before Moses" (9:11).

"And Jehovah hardened [made strong]
the heart of Pharaoh" (9:12).

7. Hail 9:13-35
JHWH said, "For this cause have I
made thee to stand, to show thee my
power, and that my name may be declared throughout all the earth" (9:16).
And ... Pharaoh ... hardened [made
heavy] his heart, he and his servants"
(9:34).

8. Locusts 10:1-20
JHWH said unto Moses, "That ye [Is-
raelites] may know that I am Jehovah"
(10:2)
"But Jehovah hardened [made strong]
Pharaoh's heart" (10:20).

9. Darkness 10:21-29
"But all the children of Israel had light
in their dwellings" (10:23).
"But Jehovah hardened [made strong]
Pharaoh's heart" (10:27).

10. Death ....11:1 to 12:36
"That ye may know that Jehovah doth
make a distinction between the Egyptians and Israel" (11:7).
Pharaoh said, "Go, serve Jehovah, as
ye have said ... bless me also" (12:31-32).

Con. Exodus and directions concerning
Passover ....12:37 to 13:16

II

Wonders Wrought for Israel Win Recognition of JHWH as Israel's God

1. At the Red Sea................13:17 to 15:21
   "Fear ye not, stand still, and see the
   salvation of Jehovah" (14:13).
   "And Israel . . . believed in Jehovah,
   and in his servant Moses" (14:31).

2. At Marah 15:22-26
   "I am Jehovah that healeth thee" (15:26)

3. At Elim and in the Wilderness
   of Sin ....15:27 to 16:36
   "I will rain bread from heaven for you
   . . . then shall ye see the Glory of Jehovah" (16:4, 7).

4. At Rephidim ....17:1 to 18:27

   (1) Water brought from the rock..17:1-7
       "Because they tempted Jehovah"
       (17:7).

   (2) Victory over Amalek.........17:8-16
       Jehovah-nissi (Jehovah is My
       Banner)" (17:15).

   (3) Visit of Jethro..............18:1-27
       "Blessed be Jehovah who hath de-
       livered you out of the hand of the
       Egyptians" (18:10).

TEXTUAL NOTES

8:27. "Three days journey" does not appear to have expressed any sort of deceit but to have been a general expression for a full journey, whatever was necessary to accomplish the purpose in view. Pharaoh evidently understood the request full well and made no charge of deceit.

12:35-36. "Asked" is correct rather than the "borrowed" of the AV. The Hebrew means either asked or borrowed. However, JHWH had told the Israelites to do this (Cf. 3:20-22). Moreover, it is indicated that the Egyptians wanted them to go (Cf. 12:33), so they "let them have what they asked."

13:21. The "pillar of cloud . . . pillar of fire" appears here for the first time. Its primary purpose appears in these words, "that they might go by day and by night." This miraculous aid thus served a very practical purpose. The result pictured in 14:30-31 shows that a yet higher purpose was the inspiration of faith. These two purposes are typical of the miraculous aid of JHWH.

It is exceedingly interesting to note that this manifestation of God is identified in 14:19-20 with the angel of God, and he is identified in the larger passage, 14:15-20, with JHWH. The purpose of his manifestation is enlarged here to include protection of Israel from enemies, indeed the whole overthrow of the Egyptians at the Red Sea, and every similar providence. The angel looms as the guardian of the chosen nation, bringing it by his plagues on its oppressors and works of wonder in its behalf to recognize him as its God (Cf. 14:30-31; 15:26; 16:4, 7; 17:5; 18:10).

16:15. The noun Manna is formed from the interrogative and personal pronouns in the question, "What is it?"

17:14. This dedication of Amalek to destruction is the first example of "holy war" in the Bible. The idea of holy war presents a moral problem to a Christian conscience and needs to be weighed carefully. At least we can note here that Amalek was thus condemned because "he met thee [Israel] by the way, and smote the hindmost of thee, all that were feeble behind thee, when thou wast faint and weary; and he feared not God."[3] His acts are judged as evidence of godless and reprobate character. Even Balaam recognized this fact.[4]

18:1-27. Moses' ideal for judgment and administration may be seen in the expression, "inquire of God," in 18:15. This ideal is magnified in the rare use of the word "gods" for judges in Exodus 21:6 and 22:8-9, describing them as representatives of God in exercise of their ideal function. The value of this ideal to a nation cannot be overestimated.

The influence of Jethro in the organization of Israel's administration must be looked upon as an

---

[3]Deut. 25:17-19.
[4]Num. 24:20.

occasion rather than a cause. In the age-enduring greatness of Moses lies the cause of Israel's system of jurisprudence, begun at Rephidim and worked out at Sinai.

A secret of Egypt's development was uniform government. Behind the prosperity of the Old Kingdom lay four centuries of united effort. The New Kingdom (2160-1788 B.C.) brought the classic period of literature, architecture, and art. The Empire (1580-1350 B.C.) restored these glories and was sustaining them in Moses' day.

This uniformity in government was not built upon the personality of a monarch merely. There was an order that maintained itself through weak reigns as well as strong, because it was built upon law. There was an extensive judicial system. All important officials were expected to know law and serve as judges when needed. There was a system of local courts throughout the land. Appeals to higher courts were in order. There were abuses, of course, but a high ideal was held up. It is described in one record thus, "judging justly, not showing partiality, sending two men [opponents] forth satisfied, judging the weak and the powerful."[5] Even the king was held to the ideal of rule by law.

This legal system and ideal of civic rights largely determined the methods by which Moses applied the principles of God to life on earth. On the other hand, there was a supremely important change in-

---

[5]Breasted, J. H., *History of Egypt*, p. 242.

troduced by Moses. He made officials responsible to God. Pharaoh was considered divine, the actual descendant of the great god Re. Therefore, the vizier who ran the government was responsible to him. Likewise, being considered divine, Pharaoh was head of the priesthood. The high priest was responsible to him. Moses recognized none but JHWH as God, and his will was the base of all law and all rights. The high priest was responsible to JHWH. Likewise, every official was responsible to JHWH.

CRITICAL PROBLEMS

VIII

Chronology of the Exodus

The length of the stay in Egypt and the date of the exodus are linked (Cf. Ex. 12:41). There are many phases of the problem and learned discussions have come down to us, as any Bible encyclopedia will testify.

Question for student investigation: Does this problem affect the spiritual and ethical value of Exodus?

ARCHEOLOGICAL SIDELIGHTS

VII

The Time of the Exodus

Parallel Reading: Price, Ira M., *MOT*, sections 107-112; 125-130; Adams, J. McKee, *BB*, pp. 115-125; Muir, James C., *HTE*, pp. 71-78; Marston, Charles, *The Bible Is True*, chapters X-XVII.

THEOLOGICAL STUDIES

XX

Hardening of Pharaoh's Heart

The hardening of Pharaoh's heart is sometimes thought of in haste as meaning that Pharaoh had no choice in the matter and so was not responsible for his deeds. In that case God's dealing with him would have been unrighteous.

Paul in Romans 9:17 points out Pharaoh's case as an example of the fact that election does not involve unrighteousness. The following facts help us to understand this reasoning: (1) during the first five plagues, Pharaoh's heart was already hard or he hardened it; (2) When JHWH hardened his heart he merely influenced him to go further in a course already chosen and unrepented of; (3) JHWH gave another opportunity for repentance in the time of the seventh plague and would surely have saved him had he given JHWH a chance to do so.

XXI

Works of Wonder

The works of wonder, or miracles, which are so prominent at this time of the exodus, are described by JHWH in Exodus 4:9 as signs. In the light of their use, we observe that they signify:

(1) The power of God. Throughout the record of the plagues we find insistence upon the purpose of JHWH to make Egyptians, Israelites, and the whole world realize that he and he alone is God, in whose hands is all power.

(2) The adoption of Israel. Beginning in the plagues, but made unquestionably clear to all in the wonders that followed, we find insistence upon the adoption of Israel by JHWH. This was expressed in a word, in Exodus 4:22, "Israel is my son, my first-born."

(3) The warning of JHWH to unbelievers. When received in unbelief, they become warnings to men like Pharaoh of the fate of men whom God gives up.

(4) The desire of JHWH to save. Throughout all records these works of wonder appear as tests of faith, providentially conceived as means of constraining men to believe. There is no power in them to make men believe, for even Israelites are not saved by them except they believe. But, they prove that God's desire to save is the central, the governing point in his use of his power, in his adoption of Israel, and in his rule of all peoples.

XXII

Passover

The sacrifice of the Passover lamb was above all else a lesson in atonement. The feast was made to be a national feast, and as such it meant a great deal to Israelites. The sacrificial meaning, however, is of universal interest.

The word of JHWH, saying, "When I see the blood, I will pass over you,"[6] is the heart of this lesson. This blood is shown to be sacrificial blood. The sprinkling of it on the doorposts and the lintel was a profession of faith in JHWH. The symbol did not save, for many who enjoyed the blessing it brought were indicated later as lost, but it was a profession of faith. Upon condition of this profession, JHWH redeemed Israelites from the bondage of Egypt. Thus the Passover, though not necessarily an experience of spiritual salvation, is a beautiful type of spiritual salvation.[7]

DETAILED OUTLINE

Theme: Making of the Covenant

I

Offer

1. Purpose: To bring Israel unto JHWH....19:1-4
2. Conditions 19:5a-b
   (1) Trust: "If ye will indeed hearken
       unto my voice" 19:5a
   (2) Obedience: "And keep my
       covenant" 19:5b

---
[6] Ex. 12:13.
[7] 1 Cor. 5:7.

3. Promises 19:5c-6

   (1) To make Israel the chosen people.19:5c

   (2) To make Israel a kingdom of
      priests 19:6a

   (3) To make Israel a holy nation....19:6b

II

Specifications

Int. Preparation for giving the law........19:7-25

1. Ten commandments: fundamental and
abiding principles of conduct or consti-
tutional law 20:1-17
(Request of the people that God speak
through Moses and instructions of
JHWH concerning an altar)...........20:18-26

2. Ordinances: relative and changing rules
of conduct, or civil law............21:1 to 23:19

3. Watchcare of the angel of the covenant,
the angel of JHWH 23:20-33

III

Ratification

1. Book of the covenant: a written, complete, and final form...................24:1-7

2. Sprinkling of blood: a sacred symbol of
mutual acceptance......................24:8

3. Feast: a celebration of the ratification...24:9-11
Con. Moses is called into the mount to re-
    ceive divinely prepared tables and in-
    structions for the people..............24:12-18

．　．　．　．　．　．　．　．　．　．　．　．　．　．

The way in which the idea of the national covenant permeates every portion of the outline makes
us to know that we come here to the climax of the
book of Exodus. The combination of discriminating
details with comprehensive analysis also makes us to
know that this is a section that is supremely important to all teaching concerning the relations of God
with his people.

．　．　．　．　．　．　．　．　．　．　．　．　．　．

TEXTUAL NOTES

19:4. "And how I bare you on eagles' wings" is
a magnificent poetic figure illustrating what the
works of wonder have done for Israel.

Deut. 32:8-11, especially verse eleven, enlarges
upon this figure:

As an eagle that stirreth up her nest,

That fluttereth over her young,

He spread abroad his wings, he took them,

He bare them on his pinions.

We see the faithful parent eagle pushing the
eaglets out of the nest as the plagues pushed Israel
out of Egypt. We can hear the little fellows squeal

as they drop from a rough and rocky pinnacle, which nevertheless has been to them a sheltered home, into a seemingly bottomless abyss, seething with uncertainties. Can it be that the old eagle no longer cares for them, no longer knows their weaknesses and fears?

We see the loving old parent bird swooping like a flash of light and taking the clinging eaglets on wings of might till they know they are not forsaken and never will be, as the crossing of the Red Sea did for Israel. Has the old eagle undertaken to carry them forever without making them learn to fly for themselves?

We see the stern and righteous parent shaking off the erratic youngsters again and again till there is born within their eagle nature a determination to do as they were created to do, to soar in the rare atmosphere of the ethereal heights, even as Israel was inspired by the wonders of the wilderness journey to do at Sinai.

"And brought you unto myself" expresses the purpose of all JHWH did hitherto for this people. It is the purpose that is now to take effect in the covenant. We need to note, however, that the nation has been merely brought "unto" JHWH, not "into" JHWH. There is an exact parallel between this expression and that used by John the Baptist and by Jesus, "The kingdom of God is at hand." Both imply that God's spiritual blessings are immediately available, but they do not take for granted that they have been appropriated. Both imply that people are being tested to see whether or not they really are the people of JHWH, whether or not they will fly as the eagle flies.

19:5. "If" tells us that the promises to follow are to be fulfilled only for those who comply with the conditions. In this case a nation is the prospective party of the second part. Faith cannot be assumed on the part of all as in the case of previous covenants with individuals. Accordingly, this "if" restricts the assurances of the covenant to those meeting the conditions.

"Obey my voice" is a description of faith rather than works, as noted in connection with Genesis 22: 18 and the faith of Abraham. Literally, it is "hearken unto my voice." It is distinguished from "Keep my covenant," which follows, so applies to the obedience of faith instead of the obedience of works. At the same time the two are inseparably linked together, as thought and deed. This helps to account for the frequent exchange of these ideas in our thinking and translations. Nevertheless, it is vital to our understanding of the teaching here to recognize that this expression makes faith to be the pivotal point in this covenant, as it is in every biblical offer of spiritual salvation.

"Keep my covenant" is the obedience we ordinarily think of as works. The verb "keep" is a synonym for "do."

These conditions are the movements that shake the eaglets from the parent's wing and challenge them to fly as the parent flies. They are moral, demanding a voluntary decision and spiritual effort. Therefore, they have spiritual results attached as promises. Those who meet these conditions are assured of the inheritance of the promises which follow. These promises are promises to Spiritual Israel as surely as those to Christians in 1 Peter 2:9. The only essential difference is that those addressed in 1 Peter 2:9 are Christians, whose faith is assumed; while those addressed here are a mixture of believers and unbelievers, whose faith must be reckoned conditionally.

"Then" points to all the promises which follow. Without exception they are assured to those who trust and obey.

Mine Own Possession

"Mine own possession" is a peculiar treasure to me or a possession especially valued by me. It describes the adoption or election of Israel as the specially chosen instrument of JHWH.

"From among all peoples" indicates the choice was free and sovereign, selecting the one instrument fitted for the purpose.

Kingdom of Priests

19:6. "A kingdom of priests" signifies a wonderful spiritual union between JHWH and his people. It tells on one hand that the people of JHWH are to be to him a priesthood. It tells on the other that JHWH is to be to his priests a king.

This priesthood of believers in turn has a double aspect. On one hand, a priest represents his people before God, leading them in worship of God. On the other hand, a priest represents God to his people, instructing them about God. Here, however, the picture rises above all ordinary ideas of priesthood. Here is envisioned a nation of priests, every member a priest. Then the other nations must be those for whom and to whom they minister. The plan of the covenant becomes universal, its purpose missionary, and its effect a blessing to all concerned.

The sovereignty of JHWH assumes a definite and practical policy, which touches all the kingdoms of this earth. This is the larger plan by which the blessing of Abraham is to be extended to all peoples. Moreover, the sovereign power of JHWH is committed to the fulfilment of it, so that the plan in no sense depends upon the sufficiency of the nation alone.

Holy Nation

"A holy nation" signifies a perfect spiritual union eventually between JHWH and his people. It describes the crowning development of the kingdom of priests as moral perfection, a people to whom has been imparted the holiness of godly character, "not having spot or wrinkle or any such thing; . . . holy and without blemish."[8]

19:8. This is the acceptance of the offer. This was the people's profession of faith or trust in JHWH.

---
[8]Eph. 5:27.

20:1 to 23:19. The law, including the ten words, or Ten Commandments as we call them, and the ordinances, specifies in detail what JHWH required of the people. As it is customary after agreement in principle concerning a contract to go into specifications, so it is done here.

23:20-33. The sending of an angel to bring Israel to the Promised Land was the guarantee of JHWH for fulfilment of his part. Thus this angel may fittingly be called the angel of the covenant.

Evidence of a Second Member of the Godhead

This angel is described as exercising the prerogatives of God, for it was said, "He will not pardon your transgression." Also he is described as possessing the character of God, for it was said, "My name is in him." Thus identified with God, he could be none other than the angel of JHWH.

A new fact concerning this angel emerges here. In that God says, "I send an angel," he distinguishes between the angel and the speaker. They are identified in purpose, character, and work, but not in person.

.   .   .   .

24:3. Here we have a second acceptance of the plans for the covenant after all specifications had been heard.

24:4-7. Here we have acceptance of written plans. Thus did Moses lead Israel into the bonds of the covenant with great care. No possible room was left for doubt about Israel's voluntary profession of faith in JHWH.

24:8. The use of blood followed the actual making of the covenant, being in no sense essential to the spiritual experience but merely a symbol of the sacred obligations imposed by it.

24:9-11. "And they saw the God of Israel" must be interpreted in the light of the context. The elders were directed to worship "afar off" (24:1). "Moses alone shall come near unto Jehovah." Then the vision of the elders could not have been as complete as that of Moses, and certainly need not be considered any more a contradiction of the teaching that "no man hath seen God at any time" than was the experience of Moses. As Moses' experiences are more clearly defined in Exodus 33:17-33, we may leave the question till we reach that point.

CRITICAL PROBLEMS
IX

Authorship of the Book of the Covenant

Brief treatments of the two sides appear in: Rule, Ulric Z., "Law in the Old Testament" in *ISBE*, pp. 1852-1854; Driver, S. R., *LOT*, pp. 30-34.

The background of these arguments may be studied in: Smith, J. M. Powis, *Origin and History of Hebrew Law;* Wilson, Robert Dick, *A Scientific Investigation of the Old Testament;* Moller, Wilhelm, *Are the Critics Right?;* Orr, James, *POT*, pp. 149-155.

Question for student investigation: Are there probable reflections of the influence of Moses throughout the Book of the Covenant? (Cf. Archeological Sidelights, No. VIII).

X
Introduction of Israel to JHWH Worship

Advocates of the documentary theories have frequently argued that Israel was introduced to JHWH at Sinai, that Sinai was thought of by the Israelites as the place of his abode, and that Moses probably learned of JHWH from the Kenite family of his father-in-law. The way in which many such theories are accepted by preachers and writers of today as facts is illustrated by "The Idea of God," in *A Guide to Understanding the Bible*, by Harry Emerson Fosdick.

General facts bearing upon the problem appear in: Oehler, Gustav F., *OTT*, pp. 96-98; Schultz, Herman, *OTT*, pp. 131-139; Davidson, A. B., *TOT*, pp. 45-58.

Question for student investigation: Would the moral integrity of the Old Testament be impaired if it should be shown that the worship of JHWH was not known in Israel before the time of the Exodus?

ARCHEOLOGICAL SIDELIGHTS
VIII
Excellence of the Mosaic Law

Parallel Reading: Price, Ira M., *MOT*, sections 130-135, 155; Price, Ira M., *MOT*, sections 136-154;

Smith, J. M. Powis, *Origin and History of the Hebrew Law.*

In what way does the Mosaic code differ from that of Hammurabi, and how may we account for the excellence of the Mosaic code?

THEOLOGICAL STUDIES

XXIII

Covenant Assurances

All provisions of the covenant are so related to each other that each is morally independent, yet each is inseparable from any other. In order to grasp all the assurances of this truth, we may picture these provisions as the stones in an arch. On one side are the provisions of man, as they appear in Exodus 19:5: (1) faith or trust, (2) works or obedience. On the other are the provisions of God as they appear in Exodus 19:5-6: (1) election, (2) kingdom of priests, (3) holiness. Though the last provision is the achievement of God's grace, it is likewise an impartation of God's character to his child. It becomes, therefore, a keystone that completes the arch, completes the trust and obedience of man as well as the election and sovereign rule of God over his priesthood. As a keystone, holiness unites, completes, and perfects all provisions of the covenant in an indissoluble union.

The infinitely meaningful assurances of this truth may be detailed as follows:

(1) Faith and election are independent yet inseparable. Every believer is elect and no believer can be lost; yet, faith does not force God to save, nor election force man to believe.

(2) As trust produces obedience, so election produces a sovereign rule of God; yet obedience remains free even as faith is free and the sovereign rule of God remains free even as election is free. These truths tell us that we are saved by faith instead of works, yet that every believer will want to serve. They likewise tell us that we are assured of salvation by election without waiting till there is complete mastery of our lives by God; yet every elect person is predestined to be subjected to the rule of God.

(3) As trust and obedience lead to holiness, so do election and the sovereignty of God. In holiness, faith and election, service and sovereignty are united, so that we can no longer distinguish them. We conclude that even in the holiness of perfection there is moral independence in both the human and divine elements; but, the union has become like a perfect sphere, and we can see only one side at a time though we know the other side is there, know moreover that the other is like the one which we behold, and no matter how many times we turn either over to look at the other the same situation remains.

Accordingly, in this plan to save unto the uttermost, appear justification by faith, the priesthood of all believers, and final perfection of the saints. These familiar concepts of New Testament theology are not so explicit as in the New Testament. Recognition of their import by many people of Israel does not appear at all. Yet, there they are in this early revelation, an eternal inspiration to the faith of men like Moses.

Parallel Reading: Schultz, Herman, *OTT*, Vol. II, pp. 1-65; Oehler, Gustav F., *OTT*, pp. 175-199; Davidson, A. B., *TOT*, pp. 235-248.

XXIV

Angel of the Covenant

God's guarantee of the fulfilment of the provisions of the covenant, as given in Exodus 23:20-33, is the angel in whom he says is his name. This can be none other than the angel of JHWH, and he may fittingly be called the angel of the covenant. He is the assurance of the assurances of the covenant.

DETAILED OUTLINE

Theme: Symbols of the Covenant

I

Tabernacle

Int. Meaning: Symbol of the dwelling of
    God with his people....................25:1-9
1. Ark 25:10-22
2. Table of shewbread 25:23-30
3. Candlestick 25:31-40
4. Curtains 26:1-6
5. Tent 26:7-14
6. Boards and bars....................26:15-30
7. Veil 26:31-35

8. Screen 26:36-37
9. Altar 27:1-8
10. Court 27:9-19
Con. Instructions concerning its keeping...27:20-21

II

Priesthood and Service

1. Garments 28:1-43
2. Consecration 29:1-37
3. Daily offering................29:38 to 30:10
4. Miscellaneous items ....30:11 to 31:11

III

Sabbath

Emulation of the rest of JHWH to remind
    Israel forever that he is "Jehovah who
    sanctifieth." 31:12-17

Conclusion

Delivery of the tables of the testimony......31:18

TEXTUAL NOTES

25:1 to 27:21. The major purpose of the tabernacle appears in 25:8, in the words, "that I may dwell among them." The word sanctuary described it merely as a place set apart or consecrated to a certain purpose. These words tell us what that purpose was. Moreover, the name tabernacle expresses that purpose because it means "dwelling."

This purpose of the tabernacle rules in the plans for every part. The ark symbolizes the conditions according to which JHWH says, "I will meet with thee, and I will commune with thee." The table of shewbread ("face-bread" or "presence-bread") appears to symbolize the presence of JHWH as the food of life. The candlestick likewise appears to symbolize the presence of JHWH as the source of life's enlightenment. All other parts likewise worked together to concentrate attention upon the meaning of the presence. The cherubim on the curtains and veil indicate this. The mere arrangement of parts taught lessons concerning approach to the presence.

In all our thinking about the tabernacle or Temple, it is quite important that we keep this major purpose clearly in view. However rich the meaning of details may be, it is not worth while except as it clarifies and magnifies the teaching concerning the major purpose. While it is necessary, as in limited lessons like the present ones, to pass over these details with no more than a reference, we may nevertheless grasp the fact that all the details are refinement of this central teaching.

These symbols are closely related to the moral and ethical teaching of JHWH worship. This appears most clearly in connection with the ark and illustrates the fact that the meaning of all the symbols arises out of their relation to the covenant. They are symbols, all of them, of the covenant relations and covenant assurances. As the ark contained the tables of the law, so it taught that the presence of JHWH was conditioned upon the people's acceptance of the law as a standard of conduct. As the ark covered the law with a mercy seat, it

taught that there was atonement for violations of
the law in the mercy of JHWH. As the cherubim
covered the mercy seat with their wings and their
faces were toward it, in sharp contrast with the cherubim guarding the way of the tree of life with a
flaming sword that turned every way, so the cherubim in this case taught that the presence or face of
JHWH was favorable to all within the covenant relations. The covenant people could seek the face of
God in confident expectation of a blessing. They
could see the cloud and fire of glory come into their
midst with rejoicing instead of fear. Above every
thing else the tabernacle was intended to signify this
favor of JHWH for the faithful.

28:1 to 30:11. The priesthood and service, as a
whole, taught the meaning of atonement. The exact
idea of the word atonement, at-one-ment, or perfect
spiritual union, is not found in any one word of the
text of Exodus or anywhere in the Bible as for that
matter, but it beautifully summarizes the following
teachings:

(1) The provision of a covering for sin.

The divisions of the tabernacle with their respec-
tive portions of equipment and ritual were designed
to symbolize a covering for sin. The outer court
could not be entered except by parties to the covenant, and then only for the purpose of delivering to
their representatives, the priests and Levites, their
offerings, the foremost of which were sin-offerings.
Into the Holy Place only the priests could enter;
and they could do so only as representatives of the

people and for the purpose of maintaining the symbols of communion which resulted from the covering of their sin. Into the holy of holies only the high priest could enter; and he could do so only as the representative of the people, only on the day of atonement (covering) and for the purpose of sprinkling the blood of atonement (covering) on the mercy seat. Thus the final and sufficient ground for atonement (covering for sin) was shown to be the mercy of JHWH.

(2) The privilege of communion with JHWH. All offerings were prayers. When the one bringing a sin-offering placed his hand on its head, acknowledging it as his substitute, his action was the equivalent of a petition that it, in its death for sin, be accepted in his stead. All other offerings symbolized some phase of prayer. The daily service at the altar of incense symbolized constant communion with the Bread of life and the Light of life, the Source of life's strength and life's enlightenment. The service on the day of atonement was an appeal to the mercy of JHWH.

(3) The assurance of holiness.

All of the following signify the assurance of holiness: the consecration of richest treasures for the making of the tabernacle; the spotless and glorious garments for those in its service; the cleanliness of body; the beauty, solemnity, and order of the ritual; the mercy seat on the ark; and above all the law of JHWH in the ark. It must ever be remembered that the mercy of JHWH is not merely a covering for violations of the law of JHWH but an assurance of the fulfilment of the law as well.

The covering, the communion, and the assurance are all included in the atonement signified by the priestly service of the tabernacle.

31:12-17. The institution of the sabbath makes sabbath observance a time symbol of covenant relations. As the tabernacle was a place, the priestly service a ritual or order, so the sabbath was a time to memorialize the people of JHWH concerning the meaning of the covenant.

The brevity of this description of the sabbath reflects the fact that the sabbath was an institution of mankind generally from the earliest times. This fact is thoroughly established by archeology also. The sabbath was here adapted to the conditions of the covenant.

CRITICAL PROBLEMS

XI

Relation of the Tabernacle to Israelitic History

Parallel Reading: Kennedy, A. R. S., "Tabernacle" in *HDB;* Whitelaw, T., "Tabernacle: B. In Criticism" in *ISBE.*

Question for student investigation: How does the critical theory of the origin of the tabernacle affect the teaching of Exodus?

ARCHEOLOGICAL SIDELIGHTS

IX

Excellence of the Mosaic Ritual

Parallel Reading: Price, Ira M., *MOT*, sections 156-159; Caldecott and Orr, "Tabernacle: A: Structure and History" in *ISBE;* Oehler, Gustav F., *OTT*, pp. 246-261; Schultz, Herman, *OTT*, pp. 65-86; Fairbairn, Patrick, *TS*, Vol. II, pp. 201-277.

In what way was the Mosaic ritual ethically superior to other ancient rituals?

THEOLOGICAL STUDIES

XXV

Atonement

(See the textual notes of Exodus 28:1 to 31:11 for a statement of the teaching.)

Parallel Reading: Carver, W. O., "Atonement" in *ISBE;* Murray, J. O. F., "Atonement" in *HDB;* Oehler, Gustav F., *OTT*, pp. 261-266; Schultz, Herman, *OTT*, pp. 87-100; Davidson, A. B., *TOT*, pp. 306-352.

DETAILED OUTLINE

Theme: Breaking and Renewal of the Covenant

I

Violation of the covenant by the making of
    the Golden Calf........................32:1-6

II

Mercy Granted

Because of Moses' pleading, JHWH consents to withhold penalty..............32:7-14

III

Wholesale Forgiveness Refused

Int. When Moses sees the licentious revelry, his anger waxes hot, he breaks the tables of the law, and he attempts expiation by leading the Levites to slaughter their brethren 32:15-29

1. His prayer that JHWH forgive, or else blot him from the book of life, is refused. 32:30-35
2. JHWH spares the people by not going in their midst 33:1-6

Con. Consequently, the tent of meeting is moved to the outside of the camp to signify that the favor of JHWH is for the seekers only 33:7-11

IV

Goodness of JHWH Explained

Int. Moses prays for understanding of ways of JHWH and that JHWH still consider Israel his people..............33:12-13

1. Pledge: to send the angel of JHWH to give Israel rest in the Promised Land for Moses' sake 33:14-17
2. Limitations 33:18-23

Int. Moses prays to see the glory of

JHWH 33:18
(1) Extension of grace and mercy lim-
    ited by the character of JHWH...33:19
(2) Revelation of God limited by abil-
    ity of man 33:20-23
3. Character 34:1-9
Int. Moses called unto Mount Sinai for
    the proclamation 34:1-6a
(1) Love: "Merciful and gracious"..34:6b
(2) Love and faithfulness: "slow to
    anger (mercy) and abundant in lov-
    ingkindness (grace) and truth
    (faithfulness)." 34:6c
(3) Love and faithfulness and right-
    eousness: "keeping lovingkindness
    for thousands (grace), forgiving ini-
    quity and transgression and sin
    (mercy and grace), and who will by
    no means clear the guilty (right-
    eousness)." 34:7
Con. Moses sees ground for renewal.....34:8-9

V

Provisions Added to Cover All Members of the Nation

1. Promise to bring the nation as a nation
   into the Promised Land................34:10a
2. Promise to accomplish the first promise by works of wonder................34:10b
3. Provision for terrible punishment of
   stubborn unbelievers 34:11-28
   (Shining and unveiling of Moses' face).34:29-35

TEXTUAL NOTES

32:6. In order to understand the tumultuous spiritual struggle of Moses in this time, we need to realize exactly the meaning of this verse. It gives an example that should stand as a naked warning to all times of the corruption of moral standards fostered by idolatry, particularly of the prostitution of chastity into which calf-worship seduced Israel in this and later times. The expression "rose up to play" describes the licentious revelry which followed the feasting and drinking as at the shrines of the gods and goddesses of fertility in Babylonia, Canaan, and elsewhere. It was this ribald scene that made Moses' anger wax hot, when he came to full realization of it, and that made him send the Levites into the camp to "slay every man his brother, and every man his companion, and every man his neighbor,"[9] because "the people were broken loose (broken away from restraint)."[10]

32:7. In describing the situation to Moses, JHWH refers to Israel as "thy people." In other words, this Israel had violated the covenant, so JHWH disowned this Israel.

Throughout the period of Moses' intercession for Israel which follows, JHWH continues to refer to the people as Moses' people or the people,[11] while Moses prays over and over that JHWH receive them

[9]Ex. 32:7.
[10]Ex. 32:25.
[11]Ex. 32:24; 33:1; 34:10, 28.

again as his people.[12]   This shows that the renewal
of the covenant is the point at issue in this time and
that an understanding of Moses' prayers with their
answers is the key to understanding of these highly
developed spiritual experiences.

32:10. "Let me alone" shows that JHWH made
his immediate handling of this people to depend
upon Moses' attitude.   This conforms to the statement in 33:17 that the renewal of the covenant was
for Moses' sake.

32:14. "Evil" here means unfortunate happen-
ing or trouble.   Accordingly, "repented of the evil"
means that JHWH consented to withhold the penalty which he would otherwise have inflicted immediately.   Moses' first prayer was a prayer for mercy,
and JHWH granted it.

32:15-19. The breaking of the tables was the
result of anger and was evidently disapproved by
JHWH, for he made Moses restore them.

32:21-29. The slaughter by the Levites likewise
received no indication of the approval of JHWH.

The anger and vengeance of Moses at this time
are easily understandable.   They are contrary to the
prayer for mercy that preceded and to the prayer
for forgiveness which came the following morning.
It was pathetic that Moses begged JHWH not to let
his wrath wax hot,[13] and then let his own break

[12]Ex. 32:12; 33:13, 16; 34:9.
[13]Ex. 32:11.

forth so violently as soon as he came in view of the actual situation. Nevertheless, these emotions are thoroughly human and understandable. They are not such touches as hero makers, creating or retouching the stories of glorified ancestors, are apt to put in. However, as conflicts in the soul of one suffering for the sins of loved ones, to the point of willingness to be damned that they might be saved, they appear natural and genuine.

32:30-35. The prayer for wholesale forgiveness was likewise contrary to the will of JHWH. Moses was doubtful about it to start with, saying, "Peradventure I shall make atonement for your sin." The refusal of JHWH to accept the offer and his very plain word, "Whosoever hath sinned against me, him will I blot out of my book," say the same thing. They do so gently but with eternal finality.

This prayer for forgiveness was in no sense a contradiction of the prayer for mercy. The prayer for mercy requested merely the withholding of penalty. The prayer for forgiveness went a long way further and begged for assurance of spiritual salvation.

This same explanation removes appearances of contradiction between 32:34 and 32:35. The notice concerning an angel to bring the people of the covenant into the Promised Land, in 32:34, was a fulfilment of the agreement to extend mercy. The warning attached, and statement of fulfilment in 32:35, were in accord with the refusal to forgive and permanently withhold punishment. Instead of being contradictions, these are illustrations of discriminating doctrinal teaching.

The prayer for forgiveness, though mistaken in its request, was also an expression of a great, great passion for the salvation of the people. It was therefore an occasion for instruction, which provoked wiser and more successful intercession.

33:5. "If I go up into the midst of them for one moment, I shall consume them" shows that it was merciful for JHWH not to manifest himself as fully to this people as Moses had desired.

33:7. "Used to take" ought to be translated proceeded to take. The verb can be translated either way, but the context shows that this action was a consequence of the explanation that preceded.

Worship of Believers Only

The place of worship came to be called "the tent of meeting," because "every one that sought Jehovah went out unto the tent of meeting." In other words, the symbolism of the tent's location was made to conform to the new situation created by the making of the Golden Calf. It is made to signify the favor of JHWH upon voluntary seekers, makers of sincere professions of faith, believers only.

33:13. "Show me now thy ways" is the prayer that opens the way for the greatest revelation of of the character of JHWH in all the experience of Moses and one of the greatest in all Old Testament history.[14]

---

[14]Ex. 33:19; 34:6-7.

"And consider that this people is thy people" is the prayer that is answered first.   This is done by the promise to send the angel of the presence, or angel of Jehovah, to bring the people into the Promised Land.[15]

33:15-17. Moses pressed JHWH for assurance that his promise meant more than a general blessing such as he stood ready to confer on any people, for assurance that it meant a special blessing, making a distinction between Israel and other nations.   The "also" of 33:17 refers to this and shows that it was granted.

33:18-23. "The glory of JHWH" appears to describe a complete manifestation of the being of God. The answer to Moses' prayer indicates that all the goodness consonant with the moral character of JHWH can and will be revealed by a proclamation of the Name, but that a complete manifestation is impossible because of man's inability to receive it. The events following on Mount Sinai fulfil both of these explanations.

Seeing God

The explanation of man's inability to comprehend all of God should be borne in mind in considering Exodus 24:10.   If one concludes that these records are the product of various minds and that contradictions in their teaching do not undermine the essential teaching of Scripture, this comparison will be for him unnecessary.   If one concludes otherwise, an understanding of 24:10 may be sought in the

---

[15]Deut. 4:37; Isa. 63:9.

teaching which appears here, that God is able to reveal himself in a limited form that is still truly God; and so man may see God without seeing all of God.

The explanation in 33:19, "And I will be gracious to whom I will be gracious, and I will be merciful to whom I will be merciful," shows that the agreement to continue working with the existing Israel as the chosen nation is limited by the character of JHWH. JHWH will be gracious and merciful to Israel but in accord with his will rather than the ideas of men, even the prayers of Moses. This is a reminder of the refusal to forgive regardless of repentance and a warning that the renewal of the covenant is not an assurance of salvation for all Israelites.

This explanation of 33:19 in the light of the prayers of Moses for the renewal of the covenant makes clear the use of it by Paul in Romans 9:15, as an illustration of the righteousness of God. Various prominent and contrary explanations, like that of Driver in *The Cambridge Bible*,[16] signally fail at this very point. The demonstration of his righteousness as a motive for the statement of JHWH appears to be conclusive reason for the explanation given.

33:19 is cryptic and hard to see through, unless we weigh the added explanation in Exodus 34:6-7. This added explanation was promised in 33:19 and expected to be an expansion of the short one.

The Proclamation of the Name in 34:6-7

The repetition of the Name shows the emphasis of the text itself.

---

[16]Driver, S. R., *The Cambridge Bible*, p. 363.

"Merciful" indicates withholding of penalty (Cf. Ps. 78:38).

"And" links mercy and grace, revealing the fullness of the love of JHWH.

"Gracious" indicates bestowal of favor. It is the positive side of love and refers to the giving of good things. Such grace can be shown to the just and the unjust. It could be shown temporarily without settling the question whether or not a soul was saved.

"Slow to anger" is a picturesque description of patience and so of mercy. Literally it is long of nostrils or slow to snort. The length in this instance is not physical length but reticence about giving vent to anger as fighters or wrestlers are wont to do by snorting.

"Lovingkindness" is at bottom simple kindness. It is also the kind of kindness that makes itself so appropriate, attractive, and beautiful as to become desired, accepted, and appropriated. It is the kindness of love and comes nearer than any other Old Testament word to being the synonym of New Testament grace.

"And" before "truth" links love with faithfulness. It tells us that JHWH not merely loves intensely but eternally.

"Truth" indicates fact, firmness, fidelity, faithfulness.

"Keeping lovingkindness for thousands" is an abbreviated form of the description JHWH gave of himself in connection with the Second Command-

ment. The full form is "showing lovingkindness
unto thousands of them that love me and keep my
commandments." This shows that the fulness of
the love and truth of JHWH can be shown only to
those who love him. For those who do love him,
however, there is lovingkindness that knows no
bounds. The word "thousands" appears to refer to
generations, in contrast with "the third and . . . the
fourth generation of them that hate me." This interpretation is confirmed by Deuteronomy 7:9. The
word thousand is a favorite symbol for perfection.
Here it is plural. Thus, this description of lovingkindness is tantamount to saying there is no bound
whatsoever to the love JHWH will show to those
who love him.

"Forgiveness" is bearing or carrying of sin. It
indicates that the love of JHWH takes the sin of
those who love him as his burden.

"Forgiving iniquity and transgression and sin" is
a parallel statement to the preceding one. Thus the
forgiveness described is the lovingkindness of
JHWH, and it is for those who love him.

"Iniquity" is error. It is a broad word covering
all sin. When distinguished from other words for
sin, it refers to the more general or less aggravated
forms of sin, as when David said, "Behold I was
brought forth in iniquity."[17]

"Transgression" is rebellion. It indicates conscious violation of known law.[18]

---

[17]Psalm 51:5.
[18]Psalm 51:3; Job 34:37.

"Sin" is habitual, hardened disobedience. As pointed out in connection with Genesis 4:7, the root means merely to miss the mark. This derivation may therefore be used to indicate a very general idea of sin which is not as strong as that of transgression.[19] General usage, however, makes this word the strongest of the words for sin, so that it is applied to the men of Sodom,[20] those who took part in Korah's rebellion,[21] the Amalekites,[22] and "the godless ones."[23]

These words for sin tell us that the forgiveness of JHWH can take up not merely the burden of iniquity but that of transgression like the worship of the Golden Calf, and not merely the burden of transgression but also that of hardened, habitual sin that has brought one to the brink of the abyss of ruin, if only the soul still loves God.

"And that will by no means clear the guilty" shows that JHWH, in the exercise of forgiveness, is both "just and the justifier of him that hath faith."[24] The "and" in this case links love and faithfulness with justice and righteousness, showing that all the attributes of JHWH are perfectly harmonized in his work of salvation. The one whose iniquity, transgression, and sin are forgiven must cease to be a "guilty" one. His forgiveness is to be accomplished, not by clearing his guilt as though it amounted to nothing or God could afford to disregard it, but by a

[19]Job 34:37.
[20]Gen. 13:13.
[21]Num. 17:3.
[22]1 Sam. 15:18.
[23]Isa. 33:14.
[24]Rom. 3:26.

righteous atonement which will maintain the standards of the righteousness of JHWH and change him
from a guilty character to a righteous character.
Not merely are the love, faithfulness, and righteousness of JHWH harmonized in his own efforts to save
the sinner, but they are finally to be harmonized in
the sinner himself.

This description of the righteousness of JHWH
is a strong repetition of what was said in the Third
Commandment, "Thou shalt not take the name of
Jehovah thy God in vain: for Jehovah will not hold
him guiltless that taketh his name in vain."[25] "Thou
shalt not take . . . in vain" means that thou shalt not
receive his name as empty, meaningless, worthless.
This shows the power of the name to depend upon
its meaning. Its power is recognized as entirely
persuasive and ethical. Its power to remove guilt is
futile in those who despise its meaning.

"Visiting the iniquity of the fathers upon the
children" goes a step further and shows that JHWH
will punish those whom his love and truth cannot
reach. Not merely will the benefits of love and truth
be denied them, but punishment will be visited upon
them. There is no prospect of universal salvation
in this, not even within Israel. This description is
also an abbreviated form of a description of JHWH
given within the Second Commandment, "For I Jehovah thy God am a jealous God, visiting the iniquity of the fathers upon the children, upon the

[25]Ex. 20:7.

third and fourth generations of them that hate me."[26] The addition of the words, "them that hate me," needs always to be kept in mind. We need to be sure to understand that this punishment which JHWH is said to visit upon fathers and children is indicated as due to hate of JHWH.

Why then are the children included in the punishment, the innocent being permitted to suffer for the guilty? Let it be observed that it is not said that the children will be condemned for their father's sins, but that they will have to suffer for them. To suffer for another's sins is a terrible thing, but it is far different from being condemned for them. The fact that they must suffer ought surely to impress the horror of sin as nothing else could. Thus the suffering of the innocent may be a means of leading them to hate sin and to love God. It may even be a means of leading others to do so. The providence that is able to so use the suffering of the innocent is just as righteous in doing so as when it causes the guilty both to suffer and to be condemned.

Though children are included, the effects are limited as a rule to the third and fourth generations, to such as may be dependent upon the guilty for the circumstances of life or come within the reach of their personal influence. This indicates a vast distinction between the extent of the influence for good by those that love JHWH and the suffering caused by those that hate JHWH. The good is the result of the mutual effort of JHWH and those who love

[26]Ex. 20:5.

him. The suffering is the result merely of the acts of the guilty. The difference is attributed to JHWH. Thus, even in the face of his stern righteousness, the overwhelming nature of his goodness bursts forth.

Especially let us note that the full statement with the entire context does not leave open the possibility of the cutting off of the love and truth of JHWH from any child, unless that child also becomes a hater of JHWH. The attitude of the individual is left as the determining factor in the salvation or condemning of that individual. Only haters of JHWH are left without hope. All lovers of JHWH are assured of salvation.

> Jehovah preserveth all them that love him:
> But all the wicked will he destroy.[27]

34:8-9. Moses saw in the proclamation of the Name the basis for renewal of the covenant. Thus he made the very fact that Israel was a stiffnecked people an occasion for JHWH to be merciful, even as the proclamation said he could be. The original form of the covenant did not make clear as to how atonement could be made for deliberate, rebellious, malicious sin, but the proclamation did, expanding the meaning of the mercy seat. The proclamation went so far as to indicate the possibility of a temporary extension of mercy and grace to unrepentant and unforgiven sinners. Therefore Moses saw in it ground for renewal of covenant relations with the nation despite its sin.

---
[27]Psalm 145:20.

34:10a. There is no if here, no offer, and no choice. All the people are included. Israelites, either by birth or circumcision, are to receive this aid regardless of trust and obedience. Thus the conditions are nonmoral, and the results are not necessarily spiritual. In other words, the beneficiaries of this promise are not necessarily saved people.

34:10b. This promise of miraculous aid is given because Israel's failure to trust and obey render the fulfilment of the former promises impossible without such aid. It is not a reward of faith but grace to the unfaithful.

34:11-28. Destruction of other nations whose iniquity will have come to the full in order to make a place for Israel will entail terrible retribution for those Israelites who stubbornly refuse to learn trust and obedience. The curses of Deuteronomy 28:15-68 are a result. The goodness of JHWH requires that he be both just and the justifier of sinners. It implies that his mercy and grace will lead to the saving of the sinner from sin or else be withdrawn eventually.

CRITICAL PROBLEMS

XII

Contradictions in the Account of Moses' Intercessions

In 32:21-29 and elsewhere confusion and contradictions appear in Moses' thinking, attitudes, and prayers. Do these contradictions discredit or strengthen the teaching about JHWH? Could

Moses have thus looked back upon his own mistakes and have thus recounted them as a lesson to others?

While acknowledging that the making of the Golden Calf is attested by the oldest sources, Kennedy says, "A very cursory examination is sufficient to show that the narrative in its present form cannot be the product of a single pen. Thus (a) the author of vv. 9-14 cannot be the author of vv. 30-34; (b) v. 35 cannot have been written by the same hand as v. 34; (c) if the chapter is a unity, the evident surprise of Moses in vv. 18-19 is inexplicable after the explanation in vv. 7-8."[28] Are these criticisms correct? Do these alleged contradictions discredit or strengthen the teaching about JHWH?

THEOLOGICAL STUDIES

XXVI

Lessons from the Name

The proclamation of the Name in Exodus 34:6-7 is the most complete description of God in the Pentateuch. It becomes a veritable touchstone of theology for the prophets of Israel. It is no wonder that Alexander Whyte said of this passage with the prayer that follows: "This passage is by far the greatest passage in the whole Old Testament. This passage is the parent passage, so to speak, of all the greatest passages of the Old Testament."[29] Outstanding among the immediate lessons given by this proclamation are:

[28]Kennedy, A. R. S., "Golden Calf," *HDB.*
[29]Whyte, Alexander, *Lord, Teach Us to Pray,* p. 52.

1. The name JHWH is a synonym for the moral perfection of God. Thus the name stands for: (a) the love of God; (b) the love and faithfulness of God; (c) the love, faithfulness, and righteousness of God, all working together in perfect harmony to manifest the holiness of God. It is with respect to this perfect moral harmony that it is said in Leviticus 19:2, "Ye shall be holy; for I Jehovah your God am holy," and in Matthew 5:48, "Ye therefore shall be perfect, as your heavenly Father is perfect."

2. The moral principles exemplified by the Name require the following distinctions as to the provisions of the covenant:

(a) The covenant assurances of Exodus 19:5-6 are for believers, only believers, and all believers in JHWH. The conditions of trust and obedience are entirely voluntary and so moral. The methods of election and the priestly kingdom are entirely spiritual in their influence, and their results therefore spiritual blessings. The purposes are corrective and perfective, leading to the impartation of holiness to every believer. This ideal part of the covenant operates according to moral and spiritual principles, which are universal; nothing forbids the inclusion of all believers regardless of race or condition; so it is open to all who would become by faith the spiritual seed of Abraham.

(b) The covenant provisions of Exodus 34:10-28 are for Israelites only, and for them whether believers or not. The conditions of birth or circumcision are not voluntary or moral. The methods of location and protection in the Land of Promise include works of wonder, and the results are not necessarily spiritual blessings. The purposes are partly punitive and destructive, including the making of the plagues wonderful upon those who enjoy the grace of God without responsive faith, and the final destruction of apostates.

3. The matchless love exemplified by the Name is the foundation of the gospel. The prophets of succeeding ages habitually turn to this description of the love of JHWH for grounds of hope that their God will succeed in saving Israel as a people. Out of their struggles over this overwhelming problem come their pictures of Messiah. Out of their pictures of Messiah, fulfilled in Jesus, New Testament evangelists weave their accounts of the full gospel story.

DETAILED OUTLINE

Theme: Institution of the Covenant Symbols

I. A freewill offering is brought until it is necessary to restrain the people from bringing ....35:1 to 36:7

II. The work is done under direction of Bezalel and Oholiab..............36:8 to 39:43

III. Erection and first use on the first day of the first month....................40:1-33

IV. Filling of the tabernacle by the glory of JHWH 40:34-38

CRITICAL PROBLEMS

XIII

Unity of Exodus

Parallel Reading: Moller, Wilhelm, "Exodus" in *ISBE;* Harford-Battersby, G., "Exodus" in *HDB;* Driver, S. R., *LOT*, pp. 20-39.

In what ways would separation into the work of several authors change the message of Exodus?

THEOLOGICAL STUDIES

XXVII

Means of Revealing the Nature of God

The spiritual nature of God is implicit throughout the Genesis and Exodus accounts. In the Second Commandment and plans for the tabernacle it is made very explicit. The commandment states this lesson; the tabernacle illustrates it. Throughout, even in the holy of holies and the ark, the tabernacle symbolizes only the moral attributes of JHWH. So it is with all other manifestations of the presence of God. In the appearance of God on Mount Sinai, Israel "heard the voice of words, but . . . saw no form."[30] Even in the appearance to Moses there was no revelation that could be described to others except the moral attributes of JHWH. All these things tell us that the essential being of God is spirit and cannot be comprehended by any physical form.

---

[30]Deut. 4:12

At the same time we are taught that God is able to assume temporary physical forms and reveal himself through them. The glory cloud in the tabernacle, the pillar of cloud and fire at any time, indeed the angel of JHWH in any form is a manifestation of the presence of God. We are prepared by the revelation of Exodus to conclude that the angel is truly God, yet the manifestation of God in him is limited to some self-chosen physical form for our sake, and that his manifestation of God is a perfect representation of God in the time and place it appears, yet not perfect in the sense of being mature and complete. The meaning of it may be progressively revealed in many other ways. What he says is the word of God, what he does is the act of God, and what he is essentially is of God; yet his present manifestations are not necessarily more than beginnings of God's revelation of himself to his children.

Parallel Reading: Wilson, Robert Dick, "Angel (II,3)" in *ISBE;* Davidson, A. B., "Angel (II)" in *HDB;* Oehler, Gustav F., *OTT,* pp. 124-144; Schultz, Herman, *OTT,* pp. 218-223.

INTRODUCTION TO LEVITICUS

Parallel Reading

Moller, Wilhelm, "Leviticus," *ISBE*

Harford-Battersby, G., "Leviticus," *HDB*

Conant, Thomas J., "Leviticus," *SBD*

Driver, S. R., "Leviticus," *LOT*

Name and Theme

The name Leviticus is another that has come from the Septuagint through the Vulgate to our English translations. The Jews followed their custom with the previous books of the Pentateuch and used the first Hebrew word, which means, "And he called." Leviticus obviously was chosen because there is so much in the book about the Levitical system and the priests. Another Jewish name, used in the Talmud, is "Law of the Priests."

The theme is closely associated with the Levitical system, but it is not that system itself. It is rather the atonement which that system is designed to promote.

Date and Authorship

Date and authorship must be considered along with that of the Pentateuch as a whole.

OUTLINE

Theme: Atonement in the Levitical System

I

Atonement Through Sacrifices

1. Burnt offerings 1:1-17
2. Meal offerings 2:1-16
3. Peace offerings 3:1-17

4. Sin offerings ....4:1 to 5:13
5. Trespass offerings ....5:14 to 6:7
Con. Directions concerning the priests' use
  of these offerings ....6:8 to 7:38

II

Atonement Through Priestly Representatives

1. Accomplished by sacrifices offered by
   truly consecrated priests............8:1 to 9:24
2. Maintained by destruction of Nadab and
   Abihu, because they offered strange fire..10:1-20

III

Atonement's Fruitage, Holiness

1. Distinction between the clean and the
   unclean ....11:1 to 15:33
2. Observance of the Day of Atonement....16:1-34
3. Refraining from eating of blood........17:1-16
4. Observance of laws of marriage, benevolence, justice, eugenics, chastity, and so
   forth ....18:1 to 20:27
5. Observance by the priests of special regulations concerning their conduct, service, and support ....21:1 to 22:33
6. Observance of the appointed seasons of
   worship ....23:1 to 24:23
7. Observance of sabbatical year and year
   of Jubilee 25:1-55
Con. Promise of blessings upon obedience
  and warning of terrible punishment for
  disobedience 26:1-46

Appendix

Laws concerning the commutation of vows. .27:1-34

TEXTUAL NOTES

In the book of Leviticus there is more than a code of laws. Throughout the discussion of the laws there is a message. Likewise in the brief historical sections and in the extended ethical teaching the same message prevails. Through all portions there runs a consistent purpose to deliver this message.

The message of Leviticus is addressed to the children of Israel. This appears in 1:2 and constantly thereafter in connection with all sections. That section concerning consecration of priests in 8:1 to 9:24 is addressed to the people as well as the priests, because the people are responsible for the procuring and support of the priests. Likewise other instructions to the priests, as in 21:1 to 22:33, are a concern of the people as well as the priests.

This message is a message concerning atonement. This appears in 1:4 and continues throughout. In 1:4 atonement appears merely as a covering for sin, an expiation of sin, and a means of reconciliation with God. The word used there is not used to describe all the sacrifices nor the holiness so magnified in the latter half of the book. However, our conception of atonement, drawn from the entire context of the covenant relations and interpreted in connection with Exodus 28:1 to 31:11, has a far greater meaning than that of the first word for atonement. This larger meaning includes communion with God and therefore the other sacrifices; likewise it includes assurance of holiness and therefore all the ethical ideas of holiness developed in the book. Emphasis upon the morally essential connection of ritual atonement with the sanctification of ethical holiness begins in 11:1-47, which comes to a climax in these words, "Sanctify yourselves therefore and be ye holy; for I am holy."[1] Over and over through the remainder of the book, especially in 18:1 to 20:27, this supreme emphasis of the message appears.

An illustration of the demand of JHWH that ritual atonement be linked with moral and ethical sanctification is found in the death of Nadab and Abihu. Their "strange fire" was a fire which JHWH "had not commanded them."[2] It represents disobedience. The injunction of JHWH to Aaron and his sons in 10:8-11 implies that the cause of the disobedience was the use of "wine" and "strong drink," which dulled their faculties so as to render them unfit to "make a distinction between the holy and the common and between the unclean and the clean," and so unfit to be teachers of the people concerning the meaning of "all the statutes" of JHWH.

Thus the message is an expanded interpretation of the atonement offered in the covenant.

The following examples of lessons from Leviticus, given by Dr. John R. Sampey, are striking illustra-

---
[1] Lev. 11:44.
[2] Lev. 10:1.

tions of the fruitage which the atonement should produce in the conduct of the godly:

(1) All offerings to God must be without blemish. He requires a perfect offering (Lev. 1:3, 10; 3:1, etc.). There was more leniency in freewill offerings, as not matters of debt, but a gift to God (Lev. 22:23).

(2) The firstfruits belong to Jehovah (Lev. 23:10). Do we put our religious offerings last of all? or does God come first?

(3) A sin unwittingly committed must be atoned for as soon as discovered (Lev. 4:2, 13, etc.).

(4) Official positions bring corresponding responsibility, the sins of rulers calling for more expensive offerings (Lev. 4:3, 22, 27, 32). Is it worse for a pastor to refuse to pay his debts than it would be for a layman? See Matthew 5:19 for the sin of false teaching.

(5) Restitution in the case of theft or other wrong must be made (Lev. 5:15, 16; 6:5; 22:14; Num. 5:6-8. Cf. Ex. 22:1-15). A professing Christian who takes the bankrupt law and afterward grows rich, without paying his debts, should be sent to school to Moses.

(6) Care should be exercised in the cultivation of a life clean in every respect (Lev. 15:31; 18:30).[3]

CRITICAL PROBLEMS

XIV

Unity of Leviticus

Parallel Reading: Moller, Wilhelm, "Leviticus," in *ISBE;* Harford-Battersby, G., "Leviticus," in *HDB;* Driver, S. R., *LOT,* pp. 39-55; Review of Exodus 28:1 to 31:11 and theological study XXV; Trumbull, Henry Clay, *The Blood Atonement.*

---

[3]Sampey, John R., *Heart of Old Testament,* p. 84f.

Are there indications within Leviticus as to the time of its composition? (Cf. 16:1; 25:1; 26:46.) Would denial of editorial supervision by Moses impair the ethical integrity of Leviticus?

ARCHEOLOGICAL SIDELIGHTS

X

Comparison of Gentile Sacrifices with Levitical

Parallel Reading: Price, Ira M., *MOT*, sections 100-103.

What practical lessons are emphasized concerning: (1) eating of swine, (2) maintenance of priests?

INTRODUCTION TO NUMBERS

Parallel Reading

Whitelaw, T., "Numbers," *ISBE*
Harford-Battersby, G., "Numbers," *HDB*
Conant, Thomas J., "Numbers," *SBD*
Driver, S. R., "Numbers," *LOT*

Name and Theme

The name Numbers has also come from the Septuagint and the Vulgate to our translations and evidently reflects the two censuses recorded in the book. The Jews have used the fifth word of the first verse, meaning "in the wilderness."

The theme is closely connected with the wilderness journeys of Israel and with the purpose which caused the censuses to be taken, but it is not clearly indicated by either name. It was the approach to the Promised Land that provoked the censuses and the journeys. As Leviticus dealt with the spiritual development promised in the covenant and described in Exodus 19:5-6, Numbers dealt with settlement in the Promised Land, as assured in Exodus 34:10-28.

Date and Authorship

Date and authorship are wrapped up in the problem of the Pentateuch as a whole.

OUTLINE

Theme: Approach to the Promised Land

I

Preparation for Journey to the Promised Land

1. Numbering and organizing of the people. 1:1 to 4-49.

2. Addition of laws concerning cleansing
   and blessing ....5:1 to 6:27
3. Offering of oblations by the princes......7:1-89
4. Purification of the Levites...............8:1-26
5. Observance of a second Passover........9:1-14
6. Explanations concerning guidance of the
   glory of JHWH......................9:15-23
7. Directions concerning trumpets to an-
   nounce journeys and assemblies........10:1-10

II

Failure to Enter the Promised Land

1. Departure from Sinai................10:11-36
2. Murmuring of the people..............11:1-35
3. Jealousy of Miriam and Aaron.........12:1-16
4. Rebellion at Kadesh-barnea and condemnation to forty years of wandering ....13:1 to 15:41
5. Rebellion of Korah..............16:1 to 17:11
6. Arrangements whereby Levites will help
   bear the iniquity of the sanctuary.17:12 to 19:22
7. Moses and Aaron forbidden to lead into
   the Promised Land because of sin at
   Meribah 20:1-13

III

Preparation for Entering the Promised Land

1. Journey from Kadesh-barnea to plains
   of Moab ....20:14 to 22:1
2. Defeat of Moab and Midian in efforts to
   curse Israel ....22:2 to 25:18

3. Listing of those to inherit the Promised
   Land ....26:1 to 27:11
4. Appointment of Joshua as Moses' successor 27:12-23
5. Regulations for offerings and vows.28:1 to 30:16
6. War with Midian 31:1-54
7. Settlement of two tribes and a half east
   of Jordan 32:1-42
8. List of Israel's stopping places.........33:1-49
9. Directions to drive out the Canaanites
   and destroy idols 33:50-56
10. Directions concerning supervisors of
    the division 34:1-29
11. Directions concerning Levites and
    cities of refuge 35:1-34
12. Directions concerning marriage of
    heiresses 36:1-13

TEXTUAL NOTES

1:1. Comparison with Exodus 40:2 shows that exactly one month had passed since the erection of the tabernacle. Thus the events recorded in Leviticus occurred in that month. Those events and all the instruction of Leviticus, like the acts and added instruction of Numbers 1:1 to 10:10, were a prepaation for the approach to the Promised Land.

11:1. The mention of murmuring in the very first word after leaving Sinai is the prelude to a long list of spiritual ills which so beset Israel as to bring about rejection of that generation of Israelites by JHWH and failure to enter the Promised Land. We find in this list murmuring, jealousy, division, and rebellion. The list gives a terrible warning as to the end to which murmuring can lead.

12:1-2. What relation was there between the fact that Moses had married a Cushite woman and the question, "Hath Jehovah indeed spoken only with Moses? hath he not spoken also with us?" Moses' marriage seems to have been more of an occasion than the real cause of the controversy. The real cause doubtless was jealousy of Moses' leadership and desire to shake off his authority.

12:4. The fact that JHWH "spake suddenly" appears to indicate that his rebuke was intended to indicate sharp displeasure with the attitude of Miriam and Aaron (Cf. 12:8b-9). They had ample opportunity to know better.

12:6-8. JHWH points out the difference between the prophetic gifts of Moses and those of the others upon whom the Spirit had rested.

This difference was what fitted Moses to be the leader. Failure to recognize this fact was what made Miriam and Aaron jealous.

Distinction as to Spiritual Gifts

The first words of JHWH, if rendered as follows, may better introduce us to his distinction between Moses and the others: In the case of your sort of prophet, I am accustomed to make myself known unto him in a vision; I am accustomed to speak unto him in a dream (12:6).

We need to note here that the vision of an ordinary prophet is described as a dream. JHWH acknowledged that he does speak through dreams, but he also indicates that that is not the best and most desirable type of revelation. In 12:8, when he says, "And not in dark speeches," he gives a further indication of his disparaging estimate. "Dark speeches" are riddles, perplexing or enigmatic sayings. In other words any means of revelation which lacks clarity and is not easily understandable is not the most desirable sort of spiritual gift.

When JHWH says of Moses, "He is faithful in all my house," he gives a very vital distinction. Moses did not prophesy for one day and do "so no more,"[1] as did the seventy. His prophesying was not spasmodic, but on duty for hard days as well as easy days, faithful all the time. Moses did not prophesy in order to claim prestige and selfish precedence. His prophesying was first of all for the sake of JHWH but also for the sake of the people of JHWH, lovingly and helpfully faithful to all concerned, seeking that which was good for all.

This faithfulness of Moses is thus marked as a fruit of his use of plain revelation, in contrast with the selfishness, littleness, jealousy, bickering, and dissension resulting from the egotism of others in their use of the "dark sayings" they had received.

There is nothing in this situation to reflect upon the truth contained in the "dark sayings." So far as the Spirit used that truth it was a blessing. The only trouble was that little souls allowed the fact that the Spirit had rested upon them in that slight degree to make "big-heads" out of them.

---

[1]Num. 11:25.

When JHWH said of Moses, "With him I am accustomed to speak mouth to mouth, even manifestly,"[2] he evidently refers to such revelation as had been given at Sinai. In this revelation are included the exalted ethical principles of the covenant, the marvelous combination of universal breadth with practical fitness found in the law, the artistic yet spiritual meaning of the tabernacle and the penetrating insight into the problems of redemption found in the proclamation of the name JHWH. Such revelations come only through reasonable communion with God, the inspiration that stimulates reason unto explanation, extension, and fulfilment of faith, while still overruling and guiding it.

How pitiful the littleness of the jealousy of Miriam and Aaron!

13:8. Hoshea was the original name of Joshua. Hoshea means Salvation. Joshua means JHWH Will Save. Likewise the names of Isaiah and Jesus carry this message. When we remember the association of Joshua with Moses in keeping the Tent of Meeting,[3] we can understand the reason for the addition in his second name, likewise his concurrence with Caleb in the minority report of the committee sent to investigate Canaan,[4] and his selection as Moses' successor.

13:26. Numbers 32:8 shows that the Kadesh mentioned here was Kadesh-barnea.

---

[2]Num. 12:8.
[3]Ex. 33:11.
[4]Num. 14:6-9.

14:39-45. There was no evidence of real willingness to obey. There was no real recognition of sin, no real repentance, only penitent crying over consequences and inconsistent determination to take affairs into their own hands. All this was conclusive evidence that they never would rightly respond to the favor of JHWH. They were rebels still and would so remain.

16:1 to 17:11. The rebellion of Korah and his followers was similar to the jealousy of Miriam and Aaron in its causes, but it went further. Where Miriam and Aaron were subject to correction, these were not. Hypocrisy and rebellion carry men and women beyond reach of the grace of God.

The budding of Aaron's rod is a part of the same story, because it was proof that JHWH did not countenance the charge of Korah that the priesthood of Aaron was not appointed by JHWH.

18:1. "Bear the iniquity of the sanctuary" is a description of the sacrificial atonement whereby the sanctity of the sanctuary was to be maintained. Violations of that sanctity had led to the deaths of Nadab and Abihu, Korah, and his followers. The people had come to fear those violations,[5] even as JHWH desired they should, so provisions are now made for ready cleansing by priests and Levites. Provision for their living was required of the people that they might devote themselves to this service.[6]

---

[5]Num. 17:12-13.
[6]Num. 18:1-32.

They in turn were made responsible for keeping at hand means of cleansing the impurity of the people.[7] "The water for impurity,"[8] made from the ashes of a red heifer, were for this purpose.

20:2-13. The sin of Moses and Aaron is revealed as: (1) unbelief, in that they failed to sanctify JHWH in the eyes of the people, which doubtless includes Moses' speaking as though he and Aaron could bring forth the water rather than JHWH;[9] (2) disobedience, in that Moses angrily struck the rock whereas he had been told to speak to it.

The stern punishment of this sin tells us that JHWH must hold his leaders to a high standard of accountability. This is necessary in order that JHWH be sanctified in the eyes of the people. It is a lesson for all leaders to remember.

21:4-9. A great lesson in faith is given here.

Looking unto the Serpent of Brass

The expression, "Looked into,"[10] can be used of trust in JHWH as in Psalms 34:5 and Zechariah 12:10. Evidently it is so used here, for repentance and request for prayer preceded.[11]

This meaning of the Serpent of Brass explains why Hezekiah destroyed it, when sight of its sym-

---

[7]Num. 19:1-22.
[8]Num. 19:9.
[9]Num. 20:10.
[10]Num. 21:9.
[11]Num. 21:7

bolic significance had been lost and it had become an idol.[12]

This meaning likewise explains why Jesus used it in explaining to Nicodemus that rebirth, or being born of the Spirit, is the same thing as believing on the crucified Christ.[13]

.   .   .   .

22:2 to 25:18. This account needs discriminating interpretation. It turns upon the character of:

Balaam

Balaam was acquainted with JHWH, for he received instructions from him.[14]

It is interesting to note in this connection that Balaam was from Pethor, "by the River,"[15] which was the Euphrates. Acquaintance with JHWH in that region is in accord with the Genesis accounts of the origin of JHWH worship.

Balaam prayed and called JHWH "my God."[16]

Balaam instructed others about JHWH.[17]

Balaam was used of God to bring assurance of salvation unto others, for the instructions just pointed out came into the hands of Israel. He even uttered a prediction of Messiah.[18]

---

[12] 2 Kings 18:4.
[13] John 3:14-15.
[14] Num. 22:12, 20, 31-33, 35.
[15] Num. 22:5.
[16] Num. 22:18.
[17] Num. 22:18, 38; 23:8-10, 19-24; 24:8-9. 13. 17-24.
[18] Num. 24:17-19.

Balaam was also covetous. Like a preacher whose conclusion as to whether or not he is called depends upon the salary, so he dealt with Balak.[19] His lofty disavowal of money seeking in 22:19 did not prevent his continuing to beg for permission to do what the Lord had plainly and positively told him not to do. The answer of JHWH was a permission but not an approval. The offer to return, which followed the opening of his eyes to see the angel of JHWH, was not accepted, because it was born of cringing, servile, obsequious fear, without reverence, love, and desire to obey. That whole experience was a warning, but Balaam was not looking for the lesson any more than he sought to find out why the ass turned aside. He was not seeking to know the will of JHWH, but to do that which this story and Jesus say is impossible, to serve both God and mammon.

Therefore, Balaam proved to be a false prophet and a lost man. His recorded prophecies were not false in their statements, because they were overruled by God. However, the prophecies were not truly his, for they were what he was compelled to say rather than what he wanted to say.[20] He is nowhere called a prophet of JHWH. He was a soothsayer as hinted by his own words in 23:23 and stated in Joshua 13:22. JHWH "turned the curse into a blessing."[21] Balaam loved not JHWH but "the hire

---

[19]Num. 22:7, 15-17; 2 Peter 2:15.
[20]Num. 23:20.
[21]Deut. 23:4; Neh. 13:2.

of wrongdoing."[22] Balaam was ethically false, so morally rotten that he "taught Balak to cast a stumblingblock before the children of Israel, to eat things sacrificed to idols, and to commit fornication."[23] His advice led to the abominations described in Numbers 25:1-18. This advice was evidently a vile means by which he tried to secure Balak's reward after JHWH had prevented his doing so with his divinations. That advice and its consequences led to Israel's war of extermination against Midian[24] and to his own death.[25]

Balaam was the Judas of the Old Testament.

Call of Joshua

27:12-23. The appointment of Joshua brings before us a character refreshingly different from that of Balaam. He was probably an officer of the people in Egypt, for he was prepared for leadership when they came out. He was appointed by Moses as general of the army at Rephidim. Moses made him keeper of the tent of meeting at Sinai. He was one of the twelve who spied out the land of Canaan and one of the two who trusted that JHWH could deliver it into the hands of Israel. He is described by JHWH as "a man in whom is the Spirit."[26] Now he is appointed to put his faith concerning the Promised Land to the test as Israel's leader in the occupation of it.

[22]2 Peter 2:15.
[23]Rev. 2:14.
[24]Num. 31:1-54.
[25]Num. 31:8.
[26]Num. 27:18.

The appointment of Joshua is as truly a divine call as that of a priest or prophet. The word used for it in 27:16 is a word which indicates that a matter is ordained. This gives, therefore, an example of the fitness of a call from JHWH to all his servants of any profession. Joshua was merely a soldier, a lay-leader in the sanctuary, and an administrator; but he was called to his work as all children of God should be.

CRITICAL PROBLEMS

XV

Unity of Numbers

Parallel Reading: Whitelaw, T., "Numbers," in *ISBE;* Harford-Battersby, G., "Numbers," in *HDB;* Driver, S. R., *LOT*, pp. 55-65.

If we take for granted, for the sake of argument, that Numbers was not written by Moses, do its historical accounts appear more or less reasonable, its ethical lessons more or less trustworthy?

ARCHEOLOGICAL SIDELIGHTS

XI

Lack of Monuments Attesting the Wilderness Wanderings

Is the failure of archeologists to find relics of Israel's life in the wilderness surprising?

THEOLOGICAL STUDIES

XXVIII

Apostasy

Outstanding examples of apostasy appear in:

1. That generation of Israelites which rebelled at Kadesh-barnea. This case is described in Numbers 14:20-23. In these verses apostates are described thus:

(1) "Those men that have seen my glory and my signs." Those men had ample opportunity to understand the character of JHWH and to trust him if they would.

(2) "Yet have tempted me these ten times." Tempting JHWH indicated doubt of him. Their continued doubt had belied their profession of faith at Sinai and had been prolonged past possibility of removal.

(3) "And have not hearkened to my voice." At bottom their trouble was an unchangeable refusal to trust JHWH.

This example of apostasy is used in 1 Corinthians 10:1-13 and Hebrews 3:12-19, as an admonition to professing Christians concerning the absolute necessity of faith.

2. Balaam. Numbers 22:2 to 25:18 reveals Balaam as one who proved in the end to be basely disloyal to JHWH, despite the fact that he had called JHWH "my God" and had prophesied in his name.

INTRODUCTION TO DEUTERONOMY

Parallel Reading

Robinson, George L., "Deuteronomy," *ISBE*

Ryle, H. E., "Deuteronomy," *HDB*

Conant, Thomas J., "Deuteronomy," *SBD*

Driver, S. R., "Deuteronomy," *LOT*

Name and Theme

The name Deuteronomy, used in Septuagint, Vulgate, and English translations, was drawn from these words in Deuteronomy 17:18, "that he shall write him a copy of this law in a book." The original text was construed in the Septuagint this way, "and he shall write for himself this repetition of the law." Its change made the repetition apply to the original work; so Deuteronomy, meaning "second law," came to be used for it. Though due to this mistranslation, the name fits reasonably after all. The book is not a second law in the sense of another law, but it is a review of the first and another interpretation of it.

The Jewish name has been the first Hebrew words, meaning "These are the words."

A yet better interpretation of the theme than that given by the name Deuteronomy may be found in the use of the words possess and possession in the book itself. These link its message with all the preceding books of the Pentateuch. Genesis gave the history of the promise concerning the Promised Land. Exodus gave the history of the covenant including that promise. Leviticus interpreted the atonement to vouchsafe that promise. Numbers gave the history of the approach to the Promised Land. Deuteronomy gives exhortations and interpretations concerning possession of the Promised Land.

Date and Authorship

The book, in 31:9, says that Moses wrote "this law." This question of date and authorship will need to be considered further in connection with the discussion of the entire Pentateuch.

OUTLINE of Deuteronomy

Theme: Possession of the Promised Land
Introduction

Note concerning author, time, and place of
  message 1:1-5

I
Call to Possess the Promised Land

1. Invitation from JHWH at Sinai.........1:6-8
2. Rebellion of former generation due to
   unbelief 1:9-46
3. Exclusion of Edom, Moab, and Ammon
   from the land to be possessed...........2:1-25
4. Conquest of Heshbon and Bashan according to command of JHWH....2: 26 to 3:11
5. Settlement of some an encouragement to
   others 3:12-22
6. Exclusion of Moses a warning to all.....3:23-29
7. Pleas for trust and obedience...........4:1-40

Appendix 4:41-49
  (1) Cities of refuge east of Jordan.4:41-43
  (2) Historical note 4:44-49

II

Pleas Concerning Conditions of Possession

Int. Explanation that the call is to the present generation upon the following conditions 5:1-2

1. Keeping always the law given at Sinai ....5:3 to 11:32
  (1) Because of promises made at Sinai ....5:3 to 6:9
  (2) Because of good things to be received in the land 6:10-25
  (3) Because of necessary separation from idolatry 7:1-26
  (4) Because of dependence taught by wilderness trials 8:1-20
  (5) Because of intercession of Moses ....9:1 to 10:22
  (6) Because of miraculous deliverance at the Red Sea............11:1-7
  (7) Because of dependence upon JHWH for rain..............11:8-25
  Con. A blessing and a curse set before them 11:26-32

2. Living as "a people holy unto Jehovah" (26:19) ....12:1 to 26:19
  (1) Organizing in the land a unified, centralized system of worship...12:1-32

(2) Destroying all who serve other
    gods ....13:1 to 14:2
(3) Observing dietary laws 14:3-29
(4) Observing labor laws 15:1-23
(5) Observing feasts of Passover,
    weeks, and Tabernacles 16:1-17
(6) Establishing justice by judges
    and kings ....16:18 to 17:20
(7) Maintaining Levites and heark-
    ening to the prophet of JHWH.18:1-22
(8) Establishing cities of refuge ...19:1-21
(9) Fearing only the word of
    JHWH in times of war........20:1-20
(10) Expiating the crimes of un-
    known murderers 21:1-9
(11) Observing miscellaneous laws
    of social justice ....21:10 to 25:19
(12) Offering unto JHWH the first-
    fruits 26:1-19

III

Explanations Concerning Consequences
of Possession

Int. Plan for proclamation of blessings
    and curses 27:1-26
1. Blessings when obedient 28:1-14
2. Curses when disobedient 28:15-68
3. Chastisements which will exile, purify,
   and permanently restore a remnant
   (Cf. 4:25-31) ....29:1 to 33:29
    (1) Covenant accepting these pro-
        visions ....29:1 to 31:13

(2) Song of Moses memorializing
Israel concerning the "expiation
for his land, for his people"
(32:43) ....31:14 to 32:47

(3) Blessing of Moses upon "Jeshurun" (33:26), the ideal national
Israel destined to enjoy complete fulfilment of the covenant ....32:48 to 33:29

Appendix: Note concerning death of Moses..34:1-12

The hortatory nature of Deuteronomy appears throughout this outline. Wherever the book deals with history or law or prophecy, it is leading to some plea for trust and obedience. In chapters 1-4 the history of the journeys between Sinai and the Promised Land leads to the pleas of 4:1-40. Those pleas set forth in principle the pleas of the entire book, but they are expanded and explained in what follows. In chapters 5-11, experiences before Sinai, at Sinai, and yet to come are pictured. In chapters 12-26, the life in the land is anticipated at every step. In chapters 27-33, disobedience, exile, and restoration are prophesied. Everywhere the purpose is to plead for trust and obedience.

TEXTUAL NOTES

4:1. The phrases, "hearken unto" and "to do them," are related to each other here exactly as faith and obedience were related to each other by similar phrases in Genesis 22:18 and in Exodus 19:5-6 (Cf. Theological Studies XIV, (2) c and XXII). They can be distinguished logically but not in practice. The whole book of Deuteronomy emphasizes this connection between true faith and a holy life.

"That ye may live and go in and possess the land" says again that possession of the Promised Land depends upon this trust and obedience. Three results are mentioned: (1) living, (2) entering the land, (3) possession of the land. Possession refers to receiving as an inheritance, as stated in 4:21. An inheritance from JHWH is looked upon in the Old Testament as a perpetual possession, even as it is written:

> Trust in Jehovah, and do good;
> Dwell in the land, and feed on his faithfulness.
>
> .   .   .   .
>
> Jehovah knoweth the days of the perfect;
> And their inheritance shall be for ever
> (Psalm 37:3, 18).

The question arises, therefore, How can the possession be perpetual yet dependent upon trust and obedience? The holding up of such a hope must prove to be a mockery for Israel unless JHWH is able to elicit from Israel an abiding trust in JHWH. Can that be?

4:25 gives the answer to our question concerning the ability of JHWH to provoke a response of abiding faith from Israel. His means for doing so are carefully enumerated. The conclusion is prophesied as an assured result, assured by the character of the God of Israel.

"In the latter days" is the time assigned for this fulfilment. These words link the fulfilment with the prophesies of Jacob in Genesis, chapter 49. That chapter links all with the work of the angel of JHWH, the Messiah who is to come.

6:4 gives a classic statement of the monotheism of the Old Testament.

"Jehovah our God is one Jehovah"

Jews, particularly since the teachings of Maimonides (A.D. 1135-1204), have interpreted the "one" as an indivisible unit in the sense of a philosophical monad. Thus they have used this verse to contradict Christian teaching concerning the Trinity.

Christians interpret the "one" as a unity with distinctions within, like those of the persons of the Godhead, harmoniously consisting. A use of the same word in this sense is found in Genesis 2:24, where it is applied to the unity including husband and wife.

12:1-32. The directions concerning a central sanctuary are often pointed out as contradicting those of Exodus 20:24-26. The directions given do certainly differ. Do they therefore indicate that those of Deuteronomy are the products of a later age and other authors than Moses? May they indicate recognition by Moses that the teachings of JHWH worship can be progressively revealed and progressively realized, even permitting relaxation of higher standards at times in view of changing circumstances?

This regulation concerning a central sanctuary is repeated in connection with the laws of tithe in 14:23, the first-born in 15:20, the feasts in 16:2, 6, 11, the judges in 17:8, 10, and the firstfruits in 26:2. Thus all the professed teaching of Moses in chapters 12-26 is brought into question by these questions concerning change in application of the laws of JHWH.

The adaptation of rules to circumstances is a matter that often vexes a Christian conscience and religious bodies. Common topics of controversy touching this problem are divorce, slavery, and conduct of women. Therefore conclusions concerning this body of teaching, professedly by Moses, are vitally related to modern and momentous questions.

The question of authorship need not determine our decision concerning the problem of change, but it will seriously affect the data available for study of the question in the Pentateuch, and it should not be dismissed as a matter of little consequence. Throughout the Pentateuch the question of authorship either saves or destroys teaching which is vital to our understanding of the meaning of JHWH worship to Moses.

If Moses wrote this interpretation of the law, he saw the principles of JHWH worship as subject to wide variations in their application to changing circumstances. For instance, he saw the question of marriage as permitting a change from the ideal of Genesis 2:23-24 to his law of divorce in Deuteronomy 24:1-4. This accords with Jesus' interpretation of Moses' law in Matthew 19:7-9. This likewise indicates the reconciliation between Moses' standard and Jesus' standard. Moses was legislating for a nation including many unbelievers and many undeveloped children of God. Jesus was giving an ideal for those who would be his disciples.

Provision for the Ministry

18:1-5. Provision of a living for the Levitical priests from the offerings is described as "the priests' due from the people." This was planned in Exodus 23:19; 30:16 and emphasized in Leviticus 22:10-16 and Numbers 18:12-19, 21. This is the right described by Paul in these words, "Know ye not that they that minister about sacred things eat of the things of the temple, and they that wait upon the altar have their portion with the altar? Even so did the Lord ordain that they that proclaim the gospel should live of the gospel."[1]

We need to observe that the Levitical priests referred to here include all that "minister about sacred things," not merely the officiating priests. In other words, this group included all whose full time was devoted to the service of God. Today the application is to laymen or laywomen who devote full time to God's service, as well as ordained ministers.

A Prophet Like Unto Moses

18:15-19 follows a plea that Israel not "hearken unto them that practise augury, and unto diviners."[2]

---

[1] 1 Cor. 9:13-14.
[2] Deut. 18:14.

It brings assurance that JHWH will not leave Israel without guidance. Therefore its promise, "JHWH . . . will raise up unto thee a prophet . . . , like unto me," can refer to many prophets which follow. At the same time, even as Genesis 49:6, 10, 24 showed that the hopes of the elect before Moses' time had begun to center upon a Coming One through whom all hopes would be fulfilled, so here the thought of Moses appears to forecast a great single prophet, or Messiah. Genesis 3:14-15 furnished a foundation for such hopes, and they continue to multiply.

Destruction of The Canaanites

20:16-18. Utter destruction of the Canaanites is said to be necessary to prevent corruption of Israel by them. This is the idea of holy war again. It does raise a serious problem for a Christian conscience and needs to be carefully considered.

First of all, we observe that it is taken for granted that these peoples were reprobate. This applies to the peoples as a whole and does not prevent the exception of individuals like Rahab of Jericho, when they show themselves desirous of becoming children of JHWH. The futility of hope for such reform on the part of many of them is shown by the parallel case in Moses' description of the Amalekites in 25:17-19.

We observe also that it is taken for granted that the purity of Israel could not be preserved unless these reprobate characters were destroyed. The fearful danger and consequences of contamination by them is shown in Numbers 25 in that "the peo-

ple began to play the harlot with the daughters
of Moab." The war of extermination against
Midian was a result of this contamination. The
war now commanded is to prevent repetition of this
contamination (Cf. Deut. 7:1-5), which was both
spiritual apostasy and physical disease as the reference to a plague in Numbers 26:1 shows.

We observe furthermore that Israel was to avoid
such terrible measures as far as possible. The context of this passage gives advice to that effect in
20:10-15. The reason for this advice would appear
to be the cultivation of compassion and tenderness
on their part as well as mercy to others.

The cultivation of compassion in this case is in
accord with compassionate measures recommended
at various places in Deuteronomy. (Cf. 15:12-17;
24:14-22.) The people are taught to have compassion on others as JHWH had compassion on them
in Egypt.

This mollifying of the severity of earlier laws in
accord with the love of JHWH is an important
example of the application of law to changing circumstances. It is a start at least toward the Christian teaching of love for enemies. Moreover, it shows
that in the thinking of Moses about the requirements of JHWH hard determination to blot out
reprobates in certain cases and tender yearning for
compassion in others are not necessarily inconsistent.
This means likewise that "going to war" under certain circumstances and "a missionary passion" under
others are not necessarily inconsistent.

Chapters 27-28. The proclamation of the blessings and the curses is an expansion of the warnings first given with the renewal of the covenant in Exodus 34:10-28 and stressed later in Deuteronomy 4: 9-33; 11:26-31. The plan that runs through all, bringing again the supreme emphasis of the covenant, appears in 28:58, "that thou mayest fear this glorious and fearful name, JEHOVAH THY GOD."

Covenant of Possession

Chapters 27-28. The proclamation of the blessings and the curses is expanded a step further in these chapters. Acceptance of that purpose by Israel is expressed by a new covenant. Though generally neglected, almost entirely so in critical discussions, this covenant gives form to a great expression of prophetic faith, second perhaps only to that first form of the covenant in Exodus 19:5-6. Its effect upon prophetical ideas of the kingdom of God appears to be tremendous. Its effect upon future history may yet be tremendous, for fulfilment of its peculiar provisions still belongs largely to the future.

This covenant may be called the covenant of possession. The first form of the Israelitic covenant was a covenant of holiness, conditioned upon faith and obedience; the second a covenant of settlement in the Promised Land, conditioned upon birth and circumcision; this one a covenant of possession of the Promised Land, conditioned not merely upon circumcision of the flesh but circumcision of the heart as well, which is to be accomplished by chastisements, including exile.

Provision for exile with all its contingencies is the most distinctive feature of this covenant of possession. This part of the purpose of JHWH was brought out in Deuteronomy 4:25-31, but not till now was it made a part of those specified provisions of the covenant which the people professed to understand and accept.

By this exile and restoration JHWH undertakes to accomplish three things: (1) purging of apostates from Israel, as described in 29:14-21, especially verses 18-21; (2) creation of an example of the work of JHWH for all peoples to see, as described in 29:22-29; (3) circumcision of "thy heart, and the heart of thy seed, to love Jehovah thy God with all thy heart, and with all thy soul, that thou mayest live" (30:6), as described throughout chapter 30.

The guarantor is JHWH. Thus it is said, "Jehovah thy God will bring thee into the land which thy fathers possessed, and thou shalt possess it" (30:5); and, "Jehovah thy God will circumcise thy heart." It is the experience of Jacob their father to be repeated in them. As JHWH revealed beforehand to Jacob's mother the election of Jacob, so he reveals here the election of a purified, permanently restored remnant of Israel. The assurance is passed on as a lesson to Gentile Christians by Paul. He speaks definitely of this in his great discussion, in Romans, chapters 9-11, of the relation of Israel to the plan of salvation by faith. He says, after acknowledging the unbelief of his "brethren according to the flesh," "But it is not as though the word of

God hath come to naught" (9:6). He goes on to show that God's promise contemplated only the salvation of a remnant. Then he concludes with this word, "For I would not, brethren, have you ignorant of this mystery, lest ye be wise in your own conceits, that a hardening in part hath befallen Israel until the fulness of the Gentiles be come in; and so all Israel shall be saved" (11:25-26a). "All Israel," as shown by the prophets later, does not mean all individual Israelites but all portions of the nation. The prophets also, with careful discussion and great emphasis, show that JHWH will make the Messiah to be his guarantee that the necessary response will be evoked from Israel's heart, even as Paul noted, quoting from Isaiah this word:

> There shall come out of Zion the Deliverer;
> He shall turn away ungodliness from Jacob:
> And this is my covenant unto them,
> When I shall take away their sins.[3]

31:14 to 32:47. The fact that the song of Moses, appearing in chapter 32, was intended as a memorial of the assurances given by the covenant of possession is shown by 31:17. Even as the people will say, "Are not these evils come upon us because our God is not among us?" so the song is to remind them that JHWH is working through these troubles "and will make expiation for his land, for his people."[4]

32:48 to 33:29. This passage, like the foregoing, is not a meaningless attachment to the main message

---

[3]Rom. 11:26, 27; Isa. 59:20f with 27:9.
[4]Deut. 32:43.

of Deuteronomy but a well planned, poetic, and prophetic peroration emphasizing the assurances of the covenant of possession. Its supreme emphasis in 33:26-29 goes on to exhaust the literary powers of Moses in praise of the God whose character vouchsafes the covenant provisions.

The supremely important item among these provisions, a future Israel transformed by the love of JHWH so as to love JHWH with all his heart, is here adorned with a new name reflecting the righteous character imparted as a gift from his God. This is Jeshurun,[5] the Straight One, the Upright One, the Righteous One, the Ideal Israel. The ending attached is used to express affection, so it might be rendered Dear Little Perfection.

CRITICAL PROBLEMS
XVI
Unity of Deuteronomy

Parallel Reading: Robinson, George L., "Deuteronomy" in *ISBE;* Ryle, H. E., "Deuteronomy" in *HDB;* Driver, S. R., *LOT,* pp. 85-96; Orr, James, *POT,* pp. 245-284; Driver, S. R., "Deuteronomy" in *ICC;* Robertson, James, *Early Religion of Israel.*

What claims does Deuteronomy make concerning its authorship? What parts of Deuteronomy would you assign to other authors than Moses? Does your division impair the ethical integrity of Deuteronomy? Do Deuteronomic changes in the law (Cf. Ex. 20:24-26; 23:14-19; 25:1-31:18; Deut. 12:1-32) indicate confusion or practical application of principle?

[5]Deut. 32:15; 33:5, 26.

XVII

Authorship of The Pentateuch

In view of the facts observed in the Pentateuch, the following opinions as to its authorship appear to be warranted:

(1) Moses was the responsible author. This view does not require that Moses wrote all that was in it, but that he directed, controlled, and was responsible for all that was in the original text. This accounts for the remarkable unity and consistency that binds the work together, especially in the interpretation of JHWH worship. Charges of confusion as in the case of Genesis 6:1-4 and of contradiction as in Exodus 6:2-3 and Exodus 32 are not admitted. Instead, the interpretation of JHWH worship is seen as a binding thread through all of it, and Moses is seen as the interpreter.

(2) Helpers like Eleazar the priest, Aaron's son, probably helped in various ways. Maybe they wrote certain passages or parts according to their own plans and styles. Such help would account for variations of style.

(3) Occasional interpolations have probably crept into the text. Explanations like that of Genesis 36:31, which mentions kings of Israel as having already reigned, appear to be additions intended to help readers of later generations understand what was in the original. These do not alter or vitiate the teaching of the original.

(4) The text has probably been damaged in a few places by the effects of wars, calamities, and the efforts of enemies to destroy the sacred writings. However, restoration by most reverent and careful handlers of the ancient manuscripts appears to have succeeded in nearly all cases in handing on to us the true sense of the original, giving to us a text that is trustworthy.

Conclusion

Obviously these opinions are contrary to the Documentary Theory of the origin of the Pentateuch. They do not deny that Moses and his helpers used both documents and traditions existing in their own day; but, they do deny that the use of *Elohim* and *JHWH,* the similarity in stories about the patriarchs, and the variations in ritual and laws arose out of conflicts between different schools of thought long after the time of Moses.

ARCHEOLOGICAL SIDELIGHTS
XII
Changes in Mosaic Law

Parallel Reading: Price, Ira M., *MOT,* sections 135-155 (Review), 164-168; Driver, S. R., "Deuteronomy" in *ICC,* pp. XXVIII-XXV; Ryle, H. E., "Deuteronomy" in *HDB,* section VII d-e.

Do the changes made by the Deuteronomic code from the codes of other people tend in any particular direction? If so, what points of law or faith seem to be their objectives? Do the changes within the Mosaic law, noted under Critical Problem XIV, tend in the same direction?

THEOLOGICAL STUDIES
XXIX
Possession of Promised Land

Possession of the Promised Land is the theme of Deuteronomy. The theological ground for assurance concerning it is outlined in the book as follows:

1. It is assured to Israel by the love of JHWH (7:6-7)
2. It is attested by the promises to the fathers (7:8)
3. It is explained by the covenant of possession (29:1 to 33:29)
   (1) As conditioned by trust and obedience (4:1; 29:10-13)
   (2) As a means in the hands of JHWH for the development of trust and obedience, according to these steps: (a) anger provoked by idolatry (4:25); (b) exile (4:26); (c) reduction to a remnant (4:27); (d) tribulation (4:28); (e) return to JHWH in faith in the latter days (4:30; 30:6); (f) mercy and faithfulness of JHWH manifested to a restored remnant (4:31a; 30:5); (g) fulfilment of the covenant (4:31b; 30:9-10).

XXX
Ethical Monotheism

The rule of JHWH over Israel and the world is profusely described in Deuteronomy. It is shown to be the rule of one God, which is monotheism. It is also shown to be according to the love, truth, and righteousness of JHWH, which constitute an ethical system. This rule of JHWH over Israel and the world is ethical monotheism and may be further analyzed as:

1. A rule which is absolute. "Jehovah our God is one Jehovah" (6:4) describes the monotheism which requires absolute unity in the government of God. Polytheism is unthinkable in connection with this teaching, except as a fiction of the minds of men (32:9; 33:26-27). No teaching about distinctions in the Godhead or changes in the law which indicate lack of harmony in a permanent or ultimate sense is permissible.

2. A rule which applies the love, truth, and righteousness of JHWH to the conduct of men in a practical manner fitted to secure their approval and appropriation. "And thou shalt love Jehovah thy God with all thy heart, and with all thy soul, and with all thy might"[6] is the response this ethical rule is designed to secure. Thus it applies its principles:

(1) Partially in beginning. Its principles are not merely in heaven but also on earth, not merely ideal but also practical, not merely fitted to the nature of God but also to the circumstances, understanding, and purposes of men. (Cf. Divorce in Deut. 24:1-4.)

(2) Progressively and consistently at all times. The principles do not change, though the applications do. The general direction of changes is toward

---

[6]Deut. 6:5; Matt. 22:37-38.

the ideals of JHWH. (Cf. directions concerning a central sanctuary in 12:5-14; 14:23; 15:20; 16:2, 6, 11; 17:8, 10; 26:2.)

(3) Perfectly in the end. (Cf. 30:6 and "Jeshurun" in 32:15; 33:5, 26.)

3. A rule exemplified in Israel. Deuteronomy 6: 6-9, as lived by faithful Israelites, not merely put on in phylacteries after a pharisaical fashion, becomes a lesson for all men. Deuteronomy 29:22-29 shows that JHWH will utilize the dispersion of Israel among the nations as a means of bringing Israel's example to the attention of all peoples. That example will include illustrations of grace, wrath, purging of apostates, chastisements, suffering for others, and sanctification, all working together to make Israel a people of whom it can be said:

Happy art thou, O Israel:
Who is like unto thee, a people saved by
   Jehovah![7]

---

[7]Deut. 33:29a.

INTRODUCTION TO JOB

Parallel Reading

Genung, John Franklin, "Job, Book of," *ISBE*
Davidson, W. T., "Job, Book of," *HDB*
Conant, Thomas J., "Job," *SBD*
Genung, John Franklin, *Epic of the Inner Life*

Name and Theme

The name is that of the hero of the book. It has been used by Jews and Gentiles alike.

The theme of the book is the triumph of faith over suffering as seen in the experience of Job.

Date and Authorship

No one, though many able men have tried, has been able to identify the author of the book. The date remains equally uncertain. Job himself is described as living under patriarchal conditions, where heads of families also acted as priests and offered the sacrifices. Thought about God likewise reflects the ideas of the time of Abraham, Isaac, and Jacob. Therefore, we choose to study the book while the background of Genesis is fresh in our minds. As to date of writing, however, the question must be left wide open. Various possibilities appear and they are scattered from the patriarchal age to the close of the Old Testament period.

Plan and Purpose

The main body of the book is poetry. Its poetry is truly sublime, justifying such exaltation as is given by Alexander R. Gordon in these words:

Here the poetical genius of Israel reaches its noblest height. In range of imagination, and sustained splendor of diction, the Book not merely stands alone in the Old Testament but takes a foremost place among the masterpieces of the world's literature.[1]

The poetry is set in a framework of prose, including the prologue in the first two chapters, the epilogue in 42:7-17, and interspersed explanations concerning speakers and circumstances. Many interpreters have thought that the main facts of the experience of Job were originally written in prose and later used by another or others who wrote the poetry. The opinion of J. F. Genung, however, to the effect that there is such close interrelation between these parts as to incline one to believe that they are the work of one great mind, appears to be the fitting one.[2]

The poetry is used to reflect the flood tides of feeling, faith, frustration, and life-enlightening revelations of God that sweep over the soul of Job in the throes of his suffering and in the ecstasies of his victory over the doubts engendered by suffering. Nothing less than the thrilling vividness and drama of an epic type of poetry could represent the swelling passions and sublime visions of such an experience. It clothes the brief, bare thoughts of the logical outline with flowing garments of imagery that make us

[1]Gordon, Alex R., *Poets of the Old Testament*, p. 202.
[2]Genung, J. F., "Job, Book of," *ISBE*, p. 1686.

appreciate the tremendous meaning of these ideas to Job and to us.

The prose is used to give plain, brief, ordinary explanations, which are necessary if the reader is to be prepared for the outbursts of poetic passion and is to draw clear conclusions as to God's relation to the trial, the doubt, the faith, and the reward of Job.

Together the poetry and the prose are complementary. Together they give a balanced and complete message, warranting the conclusion that they are both expressions of one great and faithful soul.

Tho poetry ohould be rcmcmbcred as a series of climactic experiences in the life of Job and the prose as the historical background of his story, as traced in the outline that follows:

OUTLINE OF JOB

Theme: Triumph of Faith Over Suffering

Introduction
Causes of Job's Suffering

1. Satan is permitted by JHWH to test Job.1:1-11
2. Destruction of possessions and children fails to provoke Job to sin against God......1:12-22
3. Terrible physical affliction fails to make Job renounce God 2:1-10
4. His three friends are moved by the sight of Job to silent condemnation of him......2:11-13

I

Job's Outbursts of Feeling, Faith, and Frustration
Int. Job wishes to die.....................3:1-26

1. In reply to Eliphaz' claim that God never lets the innocent perish, Job demands proof of his guilt.....................4:1 to 7:21

2. In reply to Bildad's charge that his suffering is proof of his guilt, Job longs for an umpire to judge his case................8:1 to 10:22

3. In reply to Zophar's hard assertion that he is receiving less than he deserves, Job asserts his determination to argue his case before God to the very end.......11:1 to 14:22

4. In reply to Eliphaz' sharp accusation that he is acting hypocritically, Job expresses conviction that he has a witness in heaven ....15:1 to 17:16

5. In reply to Bildad's continued predictions of doom for the wicked, Job confesses faith that his Redeemer (*Goel*) will vindicate his name on earth after he is gone....18:1 to 19:29

6. In reply to Zophar's pictures of a bitter end for sinners, Job argues that the wicked often prosper in this life..............20:1 to 21:34

7. In reply to Eliphaz' denouncement of him for heinous crimes, Job argues that God often allows the wicked to persecute the godly ....22:1 to 24:25

8. In reply to Bildad's argument that no man can be just before God, Job asks if he has helped the needy by such an argument ....25:1 to 26:14

9. When Zophar fails to speak, Job continues
to assert that his righteousness is based
upon the fear of the Lord........27:1 to 28:28

10. When all three friends remain silent, Job
solemnly and repeatedly swears that he has
not changed from the life he was living
when God watched over him for
good ....29:1 to 31:40

II
Elihu's Arguments

Int. Elihu is provoked because Job "justified
himself rather than God"; also his three
friends "had found no answer, and yet had
condemned Job" 32:1-5

1. Job's claim to innocence is unjust, he argues,
because it forgets God's purpose to use suffering so as to chasten and turn men back
to God.......................32:6 to 33:33

2. Job's argument that he is punished without
cause charges God with doing wickedness
and aids rebellion to sin..............34:1-37

3. Job's argument that he is waiting for justification claims that he is more righteous
than God, for God's unchanging judgment
is already revealed in Job's present
suffering 35:1-16

4. Job's failure to accept his suffering as chastisement is proof that he is full of
wickedness ....36:1 to 37:24

III
God's Answers to Job

1. God makes Job acknowledge that it is utterly impossible for man to understand all the works of God..............38:1 to 40:5
2. God makes Job repent of any thought that God is ever unjust or that man is able to save himself from evil powers.....40:6 to 42:6

Conclusion
Results of Job's Victory over Suffering

1. JHWH uses Job to convict his three friends of unrighteousness 42:7-9
2. JHWH blesses the latter end of Job more than his beginning.................42:10-17

TEXTUAL NOTES

1:1. "Land of Uz." (Cf. Gen. 10:23; 22:21; 36:28.)

"Job" is a name of uncertain meaning.

In Ezekiel 14:14, 20, Job is mentioned along with Noah and Daniel in such a way as to indicate that he was thought of as an historical character like the other two.

"Perfect" is parallel to "upright" in this verse. It describes "one that feared God, and turned away from evil," rather than a sinless one.

1:6. "Sons of God" describes being in fellowship with God. Presumably they are angels. When it is said, "Satan also came among them," they are distinguished from Satan. Evidently Satan was not in fellowship with God, though he did have access to him.

1:6-12. The events recorded here were not revealed to Job. Evidently the reason it was allowed to be so was God's intention to prove false the cynical criticism of Satan in 1:9. Thus it is shown that men's faith in God, despite any loss they may suffer, is the means God uses to give the lie to doubts concerning the sincerity of their faith.

2:1-6. Again the events recorded are unknown to Job. Thus the triumph of Job's faith over the agonies of physical suffering, recorded in 2:10, is God's means of defeating Satan's libel in 2:4.

2:11. "Eliphaz the Temanite" may be associated with the land of Eliphaz (Gen. 36:4) and Teman (Gen. 36:11), descendants of Esau. Thus the land of Edom is probably indicated as the scene of this story.

2:13. "And none spake a word unto him." Those who came to comfort found nothing to say, when they saw his condition. This silence was evidence, more forceful than words, pointing to their conclusion that Job's suffering was a punishment for sin.

3:1. "Cursed his day" must be understood in the light of the speech that follows. In 3:3-10 Job wishes he had never been born, in 3:11-19 that he had died at birth, and in 3:20-26 that God would let him die now. There is no effort to take control of his life out of the hands of God, but simply a loss of all desire to live.

This outburst of feeling provoked the debate that follows. Contradictory interpretations of its meaning are the center of the argument all the way from chapter 3 through chapter 37. Job's friends think it is evidence that their conclusion about Job's sin is correct. Job at every turn maintains his innocence. And, not until God answers Job is the matter settled.

The thoughts of Job's friends run somewhat as follows: this cry for death, without any confession of sin and plea for mercy, implies that Job is innocent and makes him a hypocrite. Furthermore, it implies that he condemns God for letting him suffer without just reason for it. Therefore, it is evidence that he has committed grievous sins, which he is denying, and the consequences of which he is trying to escape.

Every argument made by his friends is countered by Job with repetitions of his innocence. Prominent among these are the statements found in 6:8-9; 10:1; 13:15-16, 18; 17:13-16; 27:5; 31:5-40. This arrangement of charge and rebuttal makes the framework of the book, and each charge must be compared with its rebuttal in order to observe the progress of thought.

Thus the thought of the book wheels round and round Job's passionate cry for death until God's answers in chapters 38-40 pave the way for the conclusion.

4:7; 5:8. Eliphaz claims that God never lets the innocent perish. Then he advises Job to seek unto God. This advice implies that he needs to confess his sin and that his cry for an immediate end to his sufferings in death forgets that vital step.

6:24. Job's reply is a demand for proof that he is guilty.

8:6, 13, 20. Bildad charges that the sufferings of Job are proof of his guilt. If he were innocent, God would not let them go on.

Chapters 9 and 10. Job, in 9:11-24, says that he has no opportunity to argue his case with God. Therefore, in 9:32-35, he wishes for an umpire who would hear his side of the case and render a decision. In 10:8-17 he presses his need for such a judge by saying that God seems to have blessed him in the past for the sole purpose of destroying him now, so that he suffers the same way when he is righteous as he would if he were wicked.

11:5-6. Zophar says that Job is receiving less than he deserves.

Chapters 12 to 14. In 13:3 Job gives up hope of changing the mind of his friends and turns to God. In 13:13-28 he makes a desperate resolve to maintain his righteousness with God to the end. This leads, in 14:7-15, to an exceedingly interesting question about the possibility of God's answer coming to him after death. In 14:7-9 he cites the example of trees that sprout out again after being cut down as a reason for thinking about the possibility of man's survival. However, he observes in 14:10-12 that there is no return of man from death into life here on earth. His wish in 14:13, "Oh that thou wouldest hide me in Sheol," then raises the question of God's making a distinction between him and others in Sheol bound unto utter destruction, and so reserving him for blessing later. In 14:14-15 he shows his eager willingness to wait till then for justification.

15:5. Eliphaz comes back with a sharp accusation to the effect that his whole attitude is hypocritical.

Chapters 16 and 17. Job goes on in 16:18-21 with his consideration of justification of his name after he is dead. This time he moves from consideration of a mere possibility to assurance of a fact. In 16:19 he says plainly, "My witness is in heaven." He thinks of one provided by God who will bear testimony that will justify him. He rises on the wings of faith to the assurance that there is to be a future life and that then God will provide the justice he has withheld in this life.

18:5-21. Bildad goes on and on with predictions of doom, based upon the same suppositions with which the friends started out.

19:23-27. All this threatening, however, serves to force the soaring faith of Job higher and higher. Like an eagle which sets itself in the face of a storm, he rises completely above it. In 19:23-24 the oft-repeated wish for an enduring memorial of his claims to innocence appears again. Then, in 19:25, he goes back to the expectation of a future life and a witness in heaven, and he describes this witness as "his Redeemer."

Meaning of Redeemer (*Goel*)

The word "Redeemer," in Hebrew, is *Goel;* and it has an exceedingly rich meaning. According to

Hebrew law, the *goel* in any case was the nearest
of kin. He was responsible for redeeming his kinsman's lost opportunities for a successful life. Four
very important examples of his responsibility are as
follows: (1) in case the kinsman becomes a slave, to
redeem his freedom; (2) in case debt threatens to
overwhelm him, to redeem his homestead so as to
maintain for him and his family a proper opportunity to live and develop; (3) in case he dies without an heir, to redeem his name by marrying his
widow and rearing a son to hand on his name to
future generations; (4) in case of death at the hands
of another man, to redeem his righteous satisfaction
by acting as the avenger of blood, whose duty it was
to pursue the killer until it be proved by a trial
conducted by the Levitical priests in a city of refuge
that he had not hated aforetime, or else to act as
executioner in case the killer be found guilty.

"At last he will stand up upon the earth," affirms
Job's faith that his Redeemer will come to the earth
to furnish the memorial of his innocence for which
he so earnestly longs. This will be a vindication of
his name against the accusations of his friends. It
will redeem his righteous satisfaction from the in-
justice he now feels. This hope looks for the coming of Messiah and is a definite messianic prophecy.

.   .   .   .

"Without my flesh" means "apart from my
flesh." The parallel statement, "After my skin,
even this body, is destroyed," makes it clear that this

is the meaning here. Job is affirming his faith that in the future life he will see God.

"On my side" is one of two meanings which the words it represents could bear. The other is "for myself." And both meanings are fitting. "On my side" is parallel to "not as a stranger," and "for myself" is parallel to "mine eyes shall behold." So Job's faith is laying hold upon two more great hopes. He expects actually to see God in the future life. Also he expects God's attitude toward him then to be favorable.

"My heart is consumed within me," is an expression of the emotion that overwhelmed Job as he took his stand on the foregoing points of faith. No wonder! It had taken tremendous spiritual courage to shake off the doubts turned loose by suffering, lack of explanation from God, and the accusations of friends. It required yet higher spiritual courage to turn with readiness toward the abyss of death and to try to pierce the darkness beyond, hitherto unbroken by the light of revelation, unrelieved as yet by such experiences as his, much less the resurrection glory of Jesus. Had there been a trailbreaker before him, it would have been so much easier. He had to rely upon faith alone, simple faith that God would finally work out the thing that was right. Since men and circumstances on earth did not permit it immediately, the Redeemer would come to earth in God's good time to vindicate that right. Since Job would doubtless be already in the beyond, he himself would see God and God's works and would know them to be in his favor. These were tremendous leaps of faith. They attained to heights of conviction not attained before. No wonder his heart was flooded with ecstasy!

The problems which had plagued Job still remained after this great declaration of faith, but he had found a weapon they could not break. He and his friends continued to argue about these problems but the great crisis in Job's soul is past. He continues to parry their arguments deliberately and skilfully. He continues to sharpen the difficult angles of these problems. He reveals frankly and without restraint the frustration he feels in view of these questions which he himself cannot answer. However, with his faith fixed, all this becomes a mere intellectual discussion on one hand and on the other an exhibition of the helplessness of the human mind as it struggles alone with the grievous problems of life.

Chapter 20. Zophar presses on with the same set opinion of Job's guilt seen before and pictures the expected consequences in harsh language. In 20:5 he says that the wicked man's triumph is brief. In 20:12-19 he argues that he will come to a bitter end, because he has done things deserving bitterness; and, in 20:23, he argues that this will be accomplished by the act of God.

Chapter 21. Job denies these arguments about the fate of wicked men in general. In 21:7-16 he asks why it is that wicked men do prosper. In 21:17-26 he asks how often is it that they suffer calamity. And in 21:27-34, especially 21:30, 33, he asserts that there are wicked men who are reserved or spared in the day of calamity and die amid circumstances that are pleasing to them, with multitudes paying tribute to them at their funerals.

Chapter 22. Eliphaz, in 22:5-11, denounces Job for every sort of heinous crime he can think of, leading again in 22:23 to the reminder that repentance will bring restoration.

Chapters 23-24. Job, all the way through 23:2-12 and 24:13-25, argues that the innocent are often left by God in the merciless hands of their destroyers.

25:4. Bildad argues that no man can be just before God.

Chapter 26. In 26:2-4, Job asks Bildad what help there is for the needy in his argument, as though to say it repeated what all of them knew already. Then, in 26:14, he reminds him that these facts are the outskirts of God's ways, while the body of them remains a vast unknown.

Chapters 27-28. Zophar failed to speak when his time came. Therefore, Job continued. In 27:8-10 he sees the godless as having no hope when God takes away his soul. In other words, he may prosper in this life but not in the future life, upon which Job has now set his hope. Accordingly, he moves on in chapter 28 to a great companion truth, namely, that man can find wisdom only in the fear of God. In this he comes to the heart of all the wisdom literature, and he portrays it in magnificent poetic figures. In 28:1-11 the marvelous achievements of man in his efforts to secure the treasures of the earth are pictured; then, in 28:12-22, his utter failure to find in life or death the price of wisdom; and then, in 28:23-28, God's revelation to man of this simple but priceless truth, "The fear of the Lord, that is wisdom."

Chapters 29-31. This time all three friends remained silent; so Job again proceeded with his own line of thought. In chapters 29 and 30 he reviewed his situation at length, leading to the conclusion that in all his suffering he is the same sort of man he was when God watched over him for good. In chapter 31 he supports this claim with most solemn affirmations that he made a covenant with God and has not broken it. There are twelve of these in an unbroken series and a thirteenth later. The beginnings of them are marked by "if" in each of the following verses: 31:5, 7, 9, 13, 16, 19, 21, 24, 26, 29, 31, 33, 38. They are cast in the form of oaths and constitute Job's final and complete denial of guilt, leading to this summary statement in 31:35: "Lo, here is my signature, let the Almighty answer me."

Chapters 32-36. The speeches of Elihu start with appeals, intended to be sympathetic and helpful, which argue that God's purpose is to use suffering as a means of chastening and turning men back to God. The argument appears in 33:14-18, 23-30. However, these appeals strive to make Job confess and repent. They are based upon the same unwarranted supposition of guilt as the previous ones, and lead to the same harsh accusations. These appear in 34:36-37; 35:13-14; 36:8-11, 16-17.

38:1 to 40:5. In chapters 38 and 39 God begins to answer Job by describing various acts of God in making the wonders of nature and by asking Job if he is able to perform such wonders or to understand them. In 40:1-2 he brings the argument to a head with this question, "Shall he that cavilleth contend with the Almighty." A paraphrase of the question might be this, "Does the critic think he can match the wisdom of the Almighty." Then, in 40:4-5, Job acknowledges that it is utterly impossible for man to understand all the works of God.

40:6 to 42:6. In 40:8 God asks Job, "Wilt thou condemn me, that thou mayest be justified?" Then, in 40:9-14, he reminds Job of his lack of power to overthrow wicked men. If a man lacks the power to do that, how can he think he knows enough about the ways of God, to condemn him? Then, in 40: 15 to 41:34, God contrasts the inability of man to handle mighty beasts like behemoth, the hippopotamus, and leviathan, the crocodile, with the power of God who created both them and man. These contrasts are drawn with superb literary artistry, and they pierce the very heart of Job with the realization acknowledged by him in 42:1-6 that any thought of God ever being unjust must be repented of in dust and ashes.

42:7-17. According to 42:7-9, God used Job to convict and correct his three friends. According to

42:10-17, God blessed his latter end more than his beginning. Both of these things signify that Job had met the terrible test of his faith triumphantly and had become thereby a more useful servant of God than he could have been otherwise.

THEOLOGICAL STUDIES

XXXI

Crises in the Experience of Job

A summary of the experience of Job may be obtained by listing the crises in it. There are twelve great turning points, as follows:

1. Loss of the dearest of earthly things. Job's response to the loss of all possessions and children was this: "Jehovah gave, and Jehovah hath taken away; blessed be the name of Jehovah" (1:21). In this he was sublimely triumphant.

2. Loss of health. Job's response to the loss of health appears in this: "What? shall we receive good at the hand of God, and shall we not receive evil?" (2:10.) In this, too, he remained unshaken.

3. Loss of his friends' confidence. When Job realized that his friends had lost confidence in him, he was shaken to the very depths of his being. This provoked the cry for death in chapter 3. In this there was grave spiritual danger, because it tended toward the conclusion that God would let the innocent perish as the wicked and so be unjust in himself.

4. Longing for a mediator. The umpire for whom Job wished so longingly in 9:32-35 was de-

sired as a mediator between him and God. As God was not a man (Cf. 9:32), Job had no means of communication with him (Cf. 9:11-12), no means of securing a judgment to distinguish between his case and that of the wicked (Cf. 9:13-24). The mediator should be the medium of God's answer and a savior from the danger he now faced.

5. Determination to argue his case with God. In 13:13-19 he made a desperate resolve to argue his case with God to the end. This implied not merely an unshakable assurance of his own innocence but also a conviction that God would hear and answer his case somehow, somewhere, sometime, whether Job could foresee the way or not. This was not the scathing denunciation of one who had lost his trust in God, but the steadfast determination of one seeking confirmation of his faith.

6. Question concerning future life. In 14:13-15 he arrived at a great question, into which he was driven by his lack of hope on one side; i.e., lack of hope for an answer from God this side of the grave, and by his strong hope on the other; i.e., his hope for an answer sometime. This was a question of life beyond the grave. Could it be that in a future life the solution would appear?

7. Faith in a heavenly witness. "Even now, behold, my witness is in heaven," (16:19) was the voice of his faith affirming his conviction that God's vindication of his innocence already existed but was reserved in heaven.

8. Faith in the coming of his redeemer to earth. "My Redeemer liveth, and at last he will stand upon the earth," (19:25) was the voice of faith proclaiming the coming of the mediator, the witness, the *goel* to earth itself with God's answer.

9. Frustration due to prosperity of the wicked. In 21:4-34 he came back to the age-old problem of the prosperity of the wicked. Faith in future vindication of the innocent did not remove the fact that God does allow the wicked oftentimes to come to an end of their earthly way honored and at ease. That remains a vexation to righteous souls despite the brightness of their faith.

10. Frustration due to suffering of the innocent. In chapters 23 and 24 he went on with the agonizing problem of the suffering of the innocent. This, too, however bright may be the faith of a saint, brings a sense of frustration into the soul many times.

11. Confession of man's inability to judge the works of God. God's first answer to Job in 38:1 to 40:2 gave Job an opportunity to acknowledge in 40:4-5 his recognition of the fact that man lacks the understanding of God's works that would be necessary to enable him to pass judgment on those works. This eliminated the first danger arising out of Job's desire to die; i.e., the danger of concluding that God lets the innocent perish as the wicked. Man simply does not know enough about the matter to warrant such a conclusion.

12. Repentance of any reflections upon the justice of God. God's second answer in 40:6 to 41:34

gave Job opportunity to repent of any reflections upon the justice of God. This Job did in 42:1-6. This eliminated the companion danger in Job's desire to die; i.e., the danger of thinking that God can ever be unjust. From the viewpoint of man's exceedingly limited knowledge, he may appear unjust at times, but never is he actually so. This repentance left Job the perfect and upright servant of God that JHWH had described in the beginning. Thus Job's faith stood the test. Thus Job remained a means in God's hands of defeating Satan and reconciling others to God.

XXXII
Character of Satan

The characteristics of Satan appear as follows:

1. He is the adversary of good men. This is in accord with his name, which means adversary.

2. He is subject to control by JHWH. He has no power except what JHWH permits.

3. He is limited in power. JHWH limits his power to such ways and times as are consistent with his own will.

4. He is unable to defeat faith in God. Despite Job's ignorance of the reason for God's permitting Satan to afflict him and of the limitation set upon his power, still Job's faith routed him.

XXXIII
New View of Suffering

Job's friends evidently labored under convictions about suffering somewhat as follows:

1. All suffering is the result of sin.

2. God punishes each act of sin with a corresponding penalty.

3. Suffering, therefore, is necessarily evidence of personal guilt.

Job's experience proved that a new view of suffering should include the following along with point one of the old view:

1. The innocent do suffer in this life as well as the wicked.

2. Suffering may be used as a means of demonstrating the faith of the saints, strengthening the faith of the saints, and extending the influence of the saints.

3. Suffering, faithfully endured, defeats Satan.

XXXIV

Distinctions in Sheol

Important teachings appear concerning distinctions in Sheol between the destiny of the righteous and of the wicked. These are scattered, rather vague and illusive; yet two vital points are definitely taught, as follows:

1. Earthly distinctions disappear forever. In 3: 17-19 and 21:23-26 the kind of distinctions which Sheol removes are described as weariness or ease, captivity or freedom, smallness or greatness, servitude or mastery, physical prosperity or suffering. The fact that such earthly distinctions disappear forever is emphasized by the oft-repeated observation that no one ever returns from Sheol. (Cf. 7:9, 10:21; 16:22; 17:13, 16.)

2. Eternal distinctions are introduced. In 14:13 Job wishes to be hidden or secreted or preserved in Sheol until God's time comes for his vindication and blessing. In 19:25-27 he sees this wish fulfilled through his coming Redeemer. On the other hand, in 24:19 sinners are seen as consumed or violently taken away by Sheol. Accordingly, 26:6 gives a parallel description of Sheol in the word *Abaddon*, which means Destruction.

INTRODUCTION TO JOSHUA

Parallel Reading

Geden, A. S., "Joshua," Book of," *ISBE*
Smith, G. A., "Joshua," *HDB*
Hackett, H. B., "Joshua, Book of," *SBD*
Driver, S. R., "Joshua," *LOT*

Name and Theme

The name Joshua is used by Jews and Gentiles alike. It is intended to distinguish Joshua as the chief character of the book, not as the author.

The theme is the conquest and division of Canaan. Much is told about Joshua's life, but there is no attempt to relate it fully or to make it the central message.

Date and Authorship

There is no exact information available concerning date and authorship. The fact that the book was put in the Hebrew Bible among the "Earlier Prophets," along with the books of Samuel and Kings, indicates a belief that these books were written from the viewpoint of the prophets. That belief appears to be all that the book itself will warrant concerning its authorship.

Conclusions reached earlier concerning the authorship of the Pentateuch leave no ground for acceptance of the theory of modern criticism to the effect that Joshua is part of a Hexateuch, written as late as the eighth century B.C

Plan and Purpose

The plan is very simple. In the first twelve chapters there is a series of stories about the conquest,

and in the remaining twelve matters pertaining to
the allotments of the tribes.

The purpose is revealed in the charge of JHWH
to Joshua in 1:2-9 and the renewal of the covenant
by Joshua in 24:1-28. It is to hold Israel true to its
covenant with JHWH. The accounts of conquest
and division are so told as to remind Israel constantly of these three facts about the covenant: (1)
the land was given according to the covenant; (2)
the covenant included the law; (3) if Israel disre-
gards the law, JHWH will deliver them into the
hands of their enemies.

OUTLINE

Theme: Conquest and Division of Canaan

A

Conquest west of Jordan—Chapters 1-12
Int. Joshua commanded to possess the land..1:1-18
  I. Visit of spies to Jericho..............2:1-24
 II. Crossing of the Jordan..........3:1 to 4:24
III. Capture of Jericho..............5:1 to 6:27
 IV. Trespass of Achan.................7:1-26
  V. Capture of Ai.....................8:1-35
 VI. Treaty with the Gibeonites..........9:1-27
VII. Conquest of the remainder of the
      land ....10:1 to 11:23
Con. List of conquered Kings............12:1-24

B

Division of the Land—Chapters 13-24
Int. Preliminary matters ....13:1 to 14:15
      1. JHWH directs Joshua to allot
         the land before his death.....13:1-7

2. Explanation concerning the inheritances of Reuben, Gad, the half-tribe of Manasseh, and Levi 13:8-33

3. Hebron to be allotted to Caleb 14:1-15

I. The lot for Judah.................. 15:1-63

II. The lot for Ephraim.............. 16:1-10

III. The lot for Manasseh............. 17:1-18

(Plans made for the seven remaining tribes) 18.1-10

IV. The lot for Benjamin............. 18:11-28

V. The lot for Simeon................. 19:1-9

VI. The lot for Zebulun.............. 19:10-16

VII. The lot for Issachar.............. 19:17-23

VIII. The lot for Asher................ 19:24-31

IX. The lot for Naphtali............. 19:32-39

X. The lot for Dan.................. 19:40-48

Con. Miscellaneous matters .... 19:49 to 24:33

1. Timnath-serah given to Joshua 19:49-51

2. Message to Joshua concerning cities of Refuge and cities for the Levites .... 20:1 to 21:45

3. Conflict with the trans-Jordanic tribes 22:1-34

4. Farewell address of Joshua.... 23:1-16

5. Renewal of the covenant at Shechem 24:1-33

THEOLOGICAL STUDIES

XXXV

Salvation of Rahab

In Joshua 6:25 we are told that Rahab the harlot with her family was "saved alive" out of the destruction of Jericho. While "saved alive" indicates nothing more than physical preservation, we are told in the New Testament that she was rewarded both for faith and works. Hebrews 11:31 speaks of her faith; James 2:25 of her works. Moreover, Matthew 1:5 shows that she married into the tribe of Judah and came to be in the lineage of Jesus. Thus she is a shining example of glory imparted even to foreigners and to those guilty of scarlet sin when they become JHWH worshipers.

XXXVI

Sacredness of the Tribal and Family Allotments

JHWH's instructions in Joshua 13:6b, 7 describe the allotments of the tribes in a way to indicate sacredness. Many later scriptures, like the story of Ruth and the story of Naboth's vineyard, show that the family allotments were likewise sacred.

The word that signifies this sacredness is inheritance. JHWH said, "Divide this land for an inheritance." These allotments were not merely lots, divisions, or portions, but inheritances. The general meaning of inheritance is something given as one's own. In this case it was a gift of God. The sacredness it thus possessed imposed both upon Israel and upon God a tremendous obligation. Israel's obligation was to keep itself worthy of possession by keeping the law. Otherwise dispossession would follow as predicted in Deuteronomy 4:25-28 and Joshua 23:16. JHWH's obligation, on the other hand, was to fulfil his promises about this land by bringing Israel back to him through chastisement and back to the land as predicted in Deuteronomy 4:29-30 and in Deuteronomy 29:1-33:29. (See Theological Study XXX). Thus this inheritance comes to be treated throughout the Bible as an everlasting inheritance (Cf. Isa. 54:17; 57:13; 66:18-21; Psalm 37: 18; Jer. 31:31-40; Ezek. 48:1-35; Rev. 7:4-8).

INTRODUCTION TO JUDGES

Parallel Reading
Geden, A. S., "Judges, Book of," *ISBE*
Konig, Eduard, "Judges, Book of," *HDB*
Orger, E. R., "Judges, Book of," *SBD*
Driver, S. R., "The Book of Judges," *LOT*

Name, Theme, Date, and Authorship

Judges is much like Joshua. The name is used by Jews and Gentiles, being obviously drawn from the outstanding characters in it, and indicating nothing as to date or authorship. The theme is the history of the judges. It was written from the prophetic viewpoint, and appears in the Hebrew Bible among the "Earlier Prophets," Joshua, Judges, Samuel and Kings.

Plan and Purpose

Not much planning appears, the book being a loose collection of stories about the judges and their people. Its purpose is the same exalted one running through Joshua; i.e., to draw from the history lessons concerning the righteousness, faithfulness, and lovingkindness of JHWH that will help hold his people true to their covenant with him. The sin, the shame, the punishment, and the repentance of God's people are described over and over so as to bring out these great lessons about their God.

OUTLINE

Theme: History of the Judges

Int. Explanation of JHWH's decision not to drive out the remainder of the nations ....1:1 to 2:23

1. Historical notes concerning Israel's failure to drive out the nations 1:1-36
2. Rebuke by the Angel of Jehovah 2:1-5
3. JHWH's use of judges to test the willingness of Israel to obey him 2:6-23
 I. Othniel
    Delivered from Moab...............3:1-11
 II. Ehud
    Delivered from Moab.............3:12-30
III. Shamgar
    Smote the Philistines 3:31
 IV. Deborah and Barak ....4:1 to 5:21
    1. Destruction of Sisera and a host of Canaanites...........4:1-24
    2. Song of Deborah and Barak...5:1-31
 V. Gideon ....6:1 to 8:35
    1. Call of Gideon...............6:1-40
    2. Victory over Midian......7:1 to 8:21
    3. Rule over Israel by Gideon...8:22-35
 VI. Abimelech 9:1-57
VII. Tola 10:1-2
VIII. Jair 10:3-5
 IX. Jephthah
    Drives out the Ammonites......10:6 to 12:7
 X. Ibzan 12:8-10
 XI. Elon 12:11-12
XII. Abdon 12:13-15

XIII. Samson
Many victories over the
Philistines ....13:1 to 16:31
Con. Stories illustrating the disorder in
the days of the Judges........17:1 to 21:25
  1. The Danites move from their
     inheritance into the North
     ....17:1 to 18:31
  2. Outrageous conduct, destruc-
     tion, and partial rescue of the
     Benjamites ....19:1 to 21:25

CRITICAL PROBLEMS

XVIII

Dates and Figures in Judges

There are problems about dates and figures in
Judges which force a conservative interpreter like
A. S. Geden to search for a solution this way:

> With the system of chronology, the fig-
> ures and dates, the ethical commentary and
> inferences would seem to have no direct
> relation. The former is perhaps a later ad-
> dition, based in part at least upon tradition,
> and applied to existing accounts, in order
> to give them their definite place and suc-
> cession in the historical record.[1]

It apears impossible, in view of the limited information now available, to furnish a clear explanation. However, one area of investigation not yet
sufficiently explored is that of questions like these:

---

[1]Geden, A. S., "Judges, Book of," *ISBE*, Vol. III, p. 1774.

(1) To what extent were "round numbers" or "symbolic numbers" used in these records? (2) Does idiomatic use of words, like the Hebrew one meaning either "thousand" or "clan," play a part in the difficulties we feel here?

THEOLOGICAL STUDIES

XXXVII

God's Use of Men With Many Faults

God's use of men with many and sometimes serious faults is conspicuous in Judges. This emphasizes greatly the fact that God can use such men to do great things in spite of their faults.

This use does not condone weaknesses and errors. Barak was used in the campaign against Sisera, but the real leader was Deborah.[2] Deborah was a prophetess and judge,[3] as well as a mother in Israel,[4] and Barak depended upon her for decisions concerning the Lord's will. In other words, a leader needs such intimate contact with God as will enable him to judge for himself concerning the will of God; and, in case there is not a man who has those qualifications, God will use a woman who does. He needs both. Likewise, God's use of Jephthah need not blind our eyes to the fact that his sacrifice of his daughter was a tragedy,[5] due to a blind sense of loyalty to an oath he ought never to have taken.[6]

[2]Judges 4:8.
[3]Judges 4:4.
[4]Judges 5:7.
[5]Judges 11:30-31.
[6]Judges 11:35.

If only he had had finer spiritual insight with his loyalty, what a power he would have been! God's use of Samson need not blind us to the fact that he was sensual[7] and that he was foolish enough to reveal the secret of his strength to Delilah.[8] What a power Samson would have been had he added wisdom and loyalty to his strength and courage! Under conditions that were very bad, God was using the best man available.

XXXVIII

Dan's Departure from His Inheritance

According to the story in Judges, chapters 17 and 18, the tribe of Dan failed to occupy its appointed inheritance and moved to the north near Mount Hermon. This fact appears as a probable explanation of the omission of Dan from the list of the tribes of Israel in Revelation 7:4-8. Dan's disregard for the sacredness of his inheritance is thus judged as causing him to fail to have a full portion among the tribes of Israel participating in the kingdom of the Christ. In view of the fact that Dan is included in Ezekiel's picture of the coming kingdom,[9] it cannot be said that none out of Dan will participate. However his portion will not be a full and equal one, such as the twelve thousand of the Revelation assigns to the other tribes.

[7]Judges 16:1, 4.
[8]Judges 16:17.
[9]Ezek. 48:2, 32.

INTRODUCTION TO RUTH

Parallel Reading

Geden, A. S., "Ruth, Book of," *ISBE*
Redpath, H. A., "Ruth, Book of," *HDB*
Hackett, H. B., "Ruth, Book of," *SBD*
Driver, S. R., "Ruth," *LOT*

Name, Theme, Date, and Authorship

The name Ruth is used by all, because Ruth the Moabitess is the heroine, and later her position in the ancestry of David gives her peculiar importance. Accordingly the theme is the story of Ruth. Since her time was the time of the judges, translations of the Bible from the Septuagint on down have placed the book after Judges, and we prefer to study it in that connection. However, its position in the Hebrew Bible among the writings, the third and late section, shows that it was written late in the Old Testament period. Nothing is known about the author. The plan is that of a simple story intended to teach the blessings that came to this Moabitess by reason of her love for Israel's people and Israel's God and to explain the place of Ruth in David's line.

OUTLINE

The heart-moving developments of the story may be put in outline form, as follows:

Theme: The Making of a Moabitess into the Great-grandmother of David

1. Ruth's choice of Israel's people and Israel's God....................................1

2. Ruth's providential meeting and favor
   with Boaz 2
3. Ruth's providentially prospered proposal
   to Boaz 3
4. Ruth's providentially blessed marriage
   to Boaz 4

THEOLOGICAL STUDIES
XXXIX

The Bittersweet of Naomi's Experience

While Ruth is the heroine, the greatest character
of the Book of Ruth is Naomi. Her story will forever glorify the part a godly mother-in-law may play
in a home. Her faith won the love of Ruth, led
Ruth to God, and on from blessing to blessing. Yet
she traveled a bitter road to reach that time of rich
reward. Only the triumphant endurance of a faith
that could not be broken was sufficient. The remarkable contrast between the bitterness of her early
travail and the sweetness of her later reward may
be seen in this summary of details:

I

The Bitterness Her Faith Endured

1. Loss of income (Cf. 1:1).
2. Loss of homestead (Cf. 1:2; 4:3-6).
3. Loss of homeland (Cf. 1:2).
4. Loss of husband (Cf. 1:3).
5. Loss of children (Cf. 1:5).
6. Loss of relatives (Cf. 1:6-13).
7. Loss of pleasantness (Cf. 1:19-20).

II

The Sweetness with Which Her Faith Was Rewarded

1. Ruth becomes a worshiper of JHWH (Cf. 1:16).
2. Ruth becomes one of JHWH's people (Cf. 1:16).
3. Ruth becomes a supporter of Naomi (Cf. 2:2, 17-19).
4. Ruth becomes the wife of Boaz (Cf. 3:1-18; 4:7-12).
5. Ruth becomes the mother of Obed (Cf. 4:13-17).
6. Ruth becomes the great-grandmother of David (Cf. 4:18-22).
7. Ruth becomes the ancestress of Christ (Cf. Matt. 1:5).

INTRODUCTION TO SAMUEL

Parallel Reading

Geden, A. S., "Samuel, Books of," *ISBE*
Stenning, J. F., "Samuel, I and II," *HDB*
Abbot, Ezra, "Samuel, Books of," *SBD*
Driver, S. R., "1-2 Samuel," *LOT*

Name and Theme

In the Hebrew Bible, 1 and 2 Samuel appeared as one book, called Samuel. In the Septuagint they were separated but linked by name with each other and also with 1 and 2 Kings, the four books being called the "Books of the Kingdoms." It is true that all four are linked by the fact that they deal with the kingdom, for the theme of 1 and 2 Samuel is the establishment of the kingdom and the theme of 1 and 2 Kings is the taking away of the kingdom. Thus we may fittingly treat 1 and 2 Samuel as one book, calling it Samuel.

Date and Authorship

Both date and authorship are unknown. The viewpoint, however, is clearly that of the prophets, as in Joshua and Judges.

Plan and Purpose

The plan reflects the prophetic viewpoint constantly in comments upon the historical records. Therefore, these comments are the key verses. They reveal the interpretation of the history. As the points are put together, it becomes evident that the purpose running through this plan is not to give the history of Samuel, Saul, and David, but to interpret

[246]

the relation of these men to the establishment of the kingdom. It is shown that Samuel prepared for it, laid the foundations; Saul tried to establish it but failed; and David succeeded in establishing it.

Recognition of this plan and purpose helps us to see the divisions of the book. The first main division closes with 1 Samuel 12, because there Samuel's preparation ceases and Saul takes over as king. Samuel continues to be a prominent figure but serves to bring out the interpretation of Saul's rule. The interpretation of Saul's rule and failure continues to be the subject throughout 1 Samuel 13-31. David appears in many of these chapters, but he also serves to bring out the interpretation of Saul. Throughout 2 Samuel David's establishment of the kingdom becomes the subject. Thus, though Saul does appear in chapter 1, he serves there merely as a background for the interpretation of David's rule.

OUTLINE

(General Outline)

Theme: Establishment of the Kingdom

A. Preparation by Samuel....1 Sam. 1:1 to 12:25
B. Failure of Saul...........1 Sam. 13:1 to 31:13
C. Establishment by David..........2 Sam. 1-24

(Detailed Outline)

Preparation by Samuel

1. Dedicated to the service of the kingdom.....................1 Sam. 1:1 to 2:11
   Key verses: 1:20, 28; 2:8-10.

2. Called to be JHWH's prophet.
   ....1 Sam. 2:12 to 4:1a
   Key verses: 2:30, 35; 3:19 to 4:1a.
3. Delivers Israel from the Philistines
   ....1 Sam. 4:1b to 7:17
   Key verses: 4:10-11; 7:3-4; 11-14.
4. Anoints Saul to be king......1 Sam. 8:1 to 10:13
   Key verses: 8:3-5, 21-22; 9:15-16; 10:1.
5. Proclaims Saul as king........1 Sam. 10:14-27
   Key verses: 10:24-25.
6. Renews the kingdom ....1 Sam. 11:1-15
   Key verses: 11:11, 14-15.
7. Interprets the nature of the kingdom
   ....1 Sam. 12:1-25
   Key verses: 12:19-25.

Failure of Saul

1. Prediction of failure provoked by usur-
   pation of the priest's office......1 Sam. 13:1-15a
   Key verses: 13:13-14.
2. Overruling by the people provoked by
   a rash oath ....1 Sam. 13:15b to 14:46
   Key verses: 14:24, 27, 44-45.
3. Break with Samuel provoked by failure
   to destroy Amalek ......1 Sam. 14:47 to 15:35
   Key verses: 15:3, 20-23, 35.
4. Jealousy provoked by David's popu-
   larity ....1 Sam. 16:1 to 18:9
   Key verses: 16:13, 17-23; 17:50, 54, 58;
   18:5, 7-9.

5. Fear provoked by wise behavior of David
.............................1 Sam. 18:10-30
   Key verses: 18:12, 15, 17, 21, 25, 29.
6. Despair provoked by JHWH's deliver-
   ances of David from his hand.........
   ....1 Sam. 19:1 to 26:25
   (1) Deliverance at Jerusalem by
       help of Michal 19:1-17
   (2) Deliverance at Ramah by help of
       the Spirit 19:18-24
   (3) Deliverance at Jerusalem by help
       of Jonathan 20:1-42
   (4) Deliverance at Keilah by help
       of Abiathar ....21:1 to 23:14
   (5) Deliverance at Maon by the help
       of the Philistines 23:15-29
   (6) Deliverance at Engedi.........24:1-22
7. Deliverance at Hachilah..........25:1 to 26:25
   Suicide provoked by defeat at hands of
   Philistines ....1 Sam. 27:1 to 31:13
   Key verses: 28:16-19; 31:2-4.

Establishment by David

1. In Judah ....2 Sam. 1:1 to 3:5
   (1) After death of Saul, David is
       made king at Hebron........1:1 to 2:4a
       Key verses: 2:1, 4.
   (2) Men of Jabesh-gilead are blessed
       for burying Saul 2:4b-7
       Key verses: 2:6-7.

(3) Victory over the northern tribes
is gradually won ....2:8 to 3:5
Key verses: 2:8-9; 3:1.

2. In all Israel ....2 Sam. 3:6 to 9:13
(1) Northern tribes turn to David. 3:6 to 5:5
Key verses: 3:6, 9, 10, 17, 21; 5:1-3.
(2) Jerusalem made capital of all
Israel 5:6-16
Key verses: 5:6-7, 9, 12.
(3) Victories over the Philistines....5:17-25
Key verses: 5:17, 20, 22, 25.
(4) Ark brought to Jerusalem to cen-
tralize worship 6:1-23
Key verses: 6:1-2, 15.
(5) Line of David established forever.7:1-29
Key verses: 7:2, 8-16.
(6) Victories over many enemies....8:1-14
Key verses: 8:1-3, 13-14.
(7) Justice and righteousness exalted
for all...................8:15 to 9:13
Key verses: 8:15; 9:1, 13.

3. In the heart of the king..........2 Sam. 10-24
(1) By the rebuke of the prophet
Nathan ....10:1 to 12:15
Key verses: 12:1, 7, 10, 13-14.
(2) By the death of Bathsheba's
child 12:16-25
Key verses: 12:20, 23.
(3) By Amnon's abuse of Tamar
.......................12:26 to 13:22
Key verses: 13:21, 22.

(4) By Absalom's assassination of
    Amnon 13:23-39
    Key verses: 13:36-39.
(5) By Absalom's rebellion and death
    ....14:1 to 18:33
    Key verses: 14:1, 21, 33; 18:5, 33.
(6) By deliverance from all his
    enemies ....19:1 to 23:39
    Key verses: 19:9-10, 14, 19-20, 23, 30;
    20:22; 21:14; 22:1.
(7) By plans for seeking the forgive-
    ness of sins through sacrifice and
    worship 24:1-25
    Key verses: 24:1, 10, 18, 24, 25.

THEOLOGICAL STUDIES

XL

Meaning of the Kingdom

In the book of Samuel the following points concerning the meaning of the kingdom become supremely important: (1) the kingdom in Israel
meant the kingdom of God; (2) the success of the
human king depended upon obedience to God; (3)
failure to obey led to rejection of Saul as king. (4)
submission to the will of JHWH, even after his
great sin, led to establishment of the line of David
forever.

Samuel's interpretation of the kingdom appears
in 1 Samuel 12:1-25. It follows in the footsteps of
Moses in Deuteronomy 17:14-20. Moreover, the
whole life of Samuel was an illustration of its prin-

ciples. The lesson of his birth and dedication were summed up by his mother in these words, "For by strength [physical strength] shall no man prevail";[1] and she was evidently thinking of the power that should prevail as ruler in Israel, for she referred immediately afterward to JHWH's king and JHWH's anointed.[2] Accordingly, Samuel's prophecies, his deliverance of Israel from enemies, and all his dealings with Saul and David made obedience to God the condition upon which his leadership in the national life of Israel was built. Because of this he was able to unite the tribes of Israel as they had not been since the days of Joshua; because of this he laid the foundations of the kingdom that followed; and because of this he himself became the greatest character in Israel between Moses' day and David's. His principles of statecraft were summed up in this: "Jehovah your God was your king."[3]

The responsibility of the human king was carefully pointed out by Samuel as he turned over the reigns of government to Saul.[4] He had been appointed by JHWH.[5] If he would serve JHWH, it would be well,[6] but if not JHWH would be against him and his people.[7]

The failure of Saul and the success of David in meeting this responsibility is marked by the discriminating use in the book of Samuel of two very

[1] 1 Sam. 2:9.
[2] 1 Sam. 2:10.
[3] 1 Sam. 12:12.
[4] 1 Sam. 12:1-5.
[5] 1 Sam. 12:13.
[6] 1 Sam. 12:14.
[7] 1 Sam. 12:15.

significant descriptions, "the anointed of JHWH" and "the servant of JHWH." "The anointed of JHWH" is used to describe both as appointees of God to this high office. "The servant of JHWH" is never used of Saul, not even by Saul himself; but it is greatly magnified in the case of David, by the Lord, by David, by the prophets, and by the psalmists.

XLI

The Anointed of JHWH

The records concerning Saul and David point to the following characteristics of "the anointed of JHWH": (1) divine ordination to office; (2) Spirit-given power for the duties of office; (3) providentially protected opportunity for fulfilment of one's call to office.

The anointing oil symbolized the divine ordination. The fact that this was equally true of political leaders and religious leaders is a fact of tremendous importance.

The coming of the Spirit of JHWH upon the anointed one is frequently pointed out. In Saul's case this seems to have produced ecstatic emotions without articulate expression of any kind[8] and also the will to fight Israel's enemies.[9] In David's case it went much further and led also to the love of David and Jonathan,[10] to wise behavior under very difficult circumstances,[11] to constant seeking for the

---

[8] 1 Sam. 10:9-12.
[9] 1 Sam. 11:6-15.
[10] 1 Sam. 18:1; 20:12-17.
[11] 1 Sam. 18:14-16.

guidance of God,[12] to respect for Saul's position as
"the anointed of JHWH,"[13] to hymn writing on
many subjects,[14] to devoted planning for the temple
and its service,[15] and to prophetic insight into the
future of Israel[16]

Providential protection was given Saul even
through David whom he persecuted, by reason of
the fact that David recognized him as JHWH's
anointed. As JHWH appointed, so JHWH alone
should remove him. The wise behavior of David in
this gave Saul another chance time after time, yet
served only to drive him on from jealousy to fear,
from fear to despair, and from despair to suicide,
because he would not yield to the good purpose in
it. Thus the things planned to help him, actually
worked out his rejection as king, not merely by God,
but also by Samuel and the people. How different
with David! In the time of his great sin the long-
suffering of God finally won him and restored him,
despite the belief of many that he had sinned away
his day of grace.

Thus anointing guaranteed gracious and longsuf-
fering aid but not success. Success depended upon
the will of man to appropriate the aid of God.

XLII

The Servant of JHWH

These records concerning Saul and David indicate that "the servant of JHWH" was anointed of

[12]1 Sam. 19:18; 20:18-42; 23:7-14.
[13]1 Sam. 24:6; 26:9.
[14]2 Sam. 1:17; 22:1; 23:1.
[15]1 Chron. chaps. 22-29.
[16]Acts 2:30.

JHWH and also successful in serving JHWH, because he learned to obey. David became an outstanding example, and the following are outstanding facts in his service: (1) he made Jerusalem the capital of a united Israel; (2) he put worship at the heart of the people's life; (3) he headed the line ordained to rule Israel forever; (4) he established justice and righteousness in his realm; (5) he learned to bow his own will to God's will in all things; (6) he laid the plans for the Temple; (7) he led in preparation of a hymnbook for Israel.

The description of David as "the servant of JHWH"[17] placed him in a very highly honored line. It starts with angels;[18] it includes Abraham,[19] Isaac,[20] Jacob,[21] Moses,[22] Joshua,[23] Caleb,[24] Job,[25] Hezekiah,[26] Zerubbabel,[27] Eliakim,[28] and the prophets;[29] and it leads on to Messiah.[30]

[17] 2 Sam. 3:18; 7:5, 8, 19-21, 25-29 (plus many other instances).
[18] Job 4:18.
[19] Gen. 26:24.
[20] Gen. 24:14.
[21] Ex. 32:13.
[22] Ex. 14:31.
[23] Jos. 24:29.
[24] Num. 14:24.
[25] Job 1:8.
[26] 2 Chron. 32:6.
[27] Hag. 2:23.
[28] Isa. 22:20.
[29] 2 Kings 9:7.
[30] Isa. 49:5-7.

INTRODUCTION TO PSALMS

Parallel Reading

Sampey, John R., "Psalms, Book of," *ISBE*

Davison, W. T., "Book of Psalms," *HDB*

Conant, T. J., "Book of Psalms," *SBD*

Murray, Thomas Chalmers, *Lectures on the Origin and Growth of the Psalms.*

Delitzsch, Franz, "Introduction," *Commentary on Psalms.*

Robertson, James, *Poetry and Religion of the Psalms.*

Name and Theme

The title in the Hebrew Bible is "Book of Praises." The title "Psalms" has come to our English versions through the Septuagint. The word "psalm" in Hebrew signifies a poem to be sung to the accompaniment of stringed instruments, and this technical meaning restricts its application in the Hebrew Bible to a part of the psalms. Our usage, however, applies it to all, looking upon all as songs sung in praise of God. In this sense Psalms is the equivalent of Book of Praises, or Hymnbook.

There is no specific indication of theme. The book being a collection of separate hymns, an indication of a common theme is hardly to be expected. Any thought common to all must be broad and express the general atmosphere rather than state a specific thesis. However, the first Psalm offers a suggestion. The key word in Psalms 1 is a good key word for all of them. It is also the first word, the word "blessed"; and it stands for all the blessings poured out by JHWH upon his children. For these blessings the psalms give praise to the God of Israel.

Date and Authorship

According to records in 1 Chronicles 15:1 to 16:43 David began to organize and provide for the Levitical choir and orchestra at the time he brought the ark to Jerusalem; also he then ordained "to give thanks unto Jehovah."[1] A psalm is attached as an expression of the thanks to be given.[2] Also, in 1 Chronicles 25:1-31, we are told of the plans of David in his old age for permanent use of this choir and orchestra in connection with the Temple. 2 Samuel 22, adds the information that David composed the psalm given there in that same period of his life. When we observe that that psalm is parallel to Psalm 18:2-50, we are led to the conclusion that the collecting of hymns for the use of the Levitical choir and orchestra began in David's time, under his direction, and that he contributed psalms of his own. 2 Chronicles 29:25-30 confirms these conclusions.

The book is divided into five collections, as follows: (1) Psalm 1-41; (2) Psalm 42-72; (3) Psalm 73-89; (4) Psalm 90-106; (5) Psalm 107-150. This division gives ground for supposition that collections of psalms were made at various times.

At the end of the second collection this note appears, "The prayers of David the son of Jesse are ended." The most probable explanation is that the collection or collections made and used under

[1] Chron. 16:7.
[2] Chron. 16:8-36.

David's direction ended thus. Therefore, unless the order was generally rearranged at a later date—and there is no evidence of general rearrangement, only of the addition of a few psalms—this note indicates that the first two collections were made in David's day. Moreover, that conclusion implies the making of the last three collections later.

Psalm 102; 137 present internal evidence indicating they were written during the exile or shortly thereafter. Psalms 85 and 126 likewise reflect post-Exilic times. Thus we are brought near to the end of Old Testament history for the final work of collecting psalms, at least to the time of Ezra and Nehemiah with their great emphasis upon the preservation of Scriptures and the study of them. Many authors have argued for a final date in the interbiblical period, but no certain evidence has been found.

The following names are associated in the superscriptions with various psalms: Moses with Psalm 90; David with 3-9, 11-32, 34-41, 51-65, 68-70, 86, 101, 103, 108-110, 122, 124, 131, 133, 138-145— seventy-three in all; Asaph with 50, 73-83; sons of Korah with 42-49, 84, 85, 87; Solomon with 72, 127; Heman the Ezrahite with 88; Ethan the Ezrahite with 89. The remaining psalms are anonymous.

The phrase used in the superscriptions to associate names with certain psalms does not necessarily indicate authorship, as readers of the English text are apt to think it does. For instance, "of David," which is more literally "to David," may have any of three distinct meanings, as follows: (1) belonging to David; i.e., by right of authorship; (2) ascribed to David; i.e., by the opinion of others who thought he was the author; (3) related to David; i.e., connected with David, because the author drew his theme from the experiences and influence of David. This fact leaves us a problem in deciding what psalms David wrote, or what psalms anybody else wrote, which must be decided usually by mere probabilities or even possibilities indicated by correspondence between the psalm itself and its historical background.

Plan and Purpose

In addition to the division into five collections, the plan of the book includes superscriptions and subscriptions in addition to the text of the psalms. These have been added by others than the authors, at unknown times, in order to give information about the historical background, the tune of the song, or the instruments used in accompaniment.

As to purpose, we should distinguish between that of the authors of individual psalms and that of the collectors. The authors were seeking to give expression, as only poetry and song could do, to the truths, emotions, and purposes that filled the hearts of JHWH's people as they became conscious of his blessings. The collectors were also seeking to provide a hymnbook for Israel.

Value of Psalms for Us

The love of Bible readers everywhere for Psalms attests the great value the book has for us already.

That value, however, may be better understood and also enhanced by use of the psalms as hymns or anthems, as devotional readings, and as evidences of the faith of Israel in JHWH. In any of these ways the arrangement and study of them after the fashion of song-sermons can be very helpful.

The following studies are arranged in accord with this suggestion about song-sermons or psalm-sermons. Selected psalms, the teaching of which is the key to a group of psalms, are studied with care. Their themes and outlines are worked out in accord with thorough exegesis. This exegesis cannot be given here, but outlines are based upon it. Then a brief exposition is given of some great doctrine lying close to the heart of each. Any of these could of course be greatly enlarged, but that enlargement cannot be undertaken here. Moreover, an attempt is made to link these theological studies in such a way as to give an impression of the great range of truth in Israel's faith as reflected in their hymns. This view can give us glimpses only, but it may inspire determination to climb the heights themselves.

LIST OF STUDIES IN SELECTED PSALMS

Theme: Blessings in Psalms

Int. A Contrast of the Righteous and the
        Wicked ....Psalm 1
A.   The Blessing of Messiah's Control over
        the Nations ....Psalm 2
B.   The Blessing of Messiah's Control over
        Enemies ....Psalm 18

C. The Blessing of Messiah's Control over
    Death ....Psalm 22
D. The Blessing of Messiah's Control over
    the King ....Psalm 23
E. The Blessing of Worship...........Psalm 29
F. The Blessing of Forgiveness........Psalm 32
G. The Blessing of Prayer............Psalm 51
H. The Blessing of Missions..........Psalm 67
I. The Blessing of Succession.........Psalm 72
J. The Blessing of Assurance.........Psalm 73
K. The Blessing of Praise...........Psalm 103
L. The Blessing of Messiah's Control over
    the World ....Psalm 110

.   .   .   .

A Contrast of the Righteous and the Wicked

OUTLINE OF PSALM 1

Theme: The Righteous and the Wicked

I

The Righteous

1. Blessed 1:1
2. Happy 1:2
3. Fruitful 1:3

II

The Wicked

1. Worthless 1:4
2. Unstable 1:5
3. Doomed 1:6

THEOLOGICAL STUDIES

XLII

Meaning of Blessed

Some of the earliest Old Testament manuscripts begin the book of Psalms with Psalm 2. A reasonable deduction is that Psalm 1 was put in its present position when later editions appeared. Probably this was done because it furnished an introduction to the book. A careful examination of its message supports this conclusion. Within the broad outlines of its pictures of the righteous and the wicked all the other messages of the book may be fittingly placed.

"Blessed," the first word of Psalm 1, is a word that fits the introductory purpose of the psalm perfectly. It is so rich in meaning that it covers all the blessings in Psalms. It may be called the key word in Psalms.

In the original text "blessed" is a plural noun. One idea conveyed by this plural is that there are many blessings bestowed by Jehovah upon the righteous. Accordingly, all the psalms praise God for the multitude of his blessings. However, there is a yet greater significance in this plural. Like many other Hebrew plurals, as, for instance, the name *Elohim* (God), which signifies the fulness of God's power, so this plural may signify the fulness or plentitude of the blessings which God bestows.

Another fact about the original word for blessed, another one not apparent in the translation, is that it was part of an exclamation. The translation would be better this way:

> Oh, the fulness of the blessings
> belonging to the man that walk-
> eth not in the counsel of the
> wicked!

This exclamation expresses the feeling of a heart that has been stirred to its depths by comtempla-tion of the blessings bestowed upon it by the Lord. This is the kind of feeling that surges through all the psalms. That is why they are written in poetry. That is why they command such vividness of illus-tration, such beauty of words, such elegance of thought. As a heart-seeking expression for its first love turns to poetry, so the hearts of the psalmists burst out in exclamations of praise. Surely it is true that all the children of God dearly love the psalms because they find in them expressions of the deepest emotion of their own hearts.

This word is the same word used over and over by Jesus in the Beatitudes. Even as it is a fervent pronouncement upon all the good envisioned there, so it is in Psalms.

It is indeed the initial outburst of paeans of praise.

THEOLOGICAL STUDIES

(In Outline)

XLIV

Nature, Identity, and Destiny of the Blessed

1. Nature of the blessed:

Not righteous in God's sight; i.e., of themselves.

143:2b.

One whose soul thirsteth for God. 1:2; 143:6b.

One who trusts in JHWH. 143:8b.

One who prays to be taught God's will for him. 143:10a.

One who accepts the salvation of JHWH. 116: 12-13.

One who depends upon God to give him righteousness. 24:5; 19:13-14.

One whose habits are consistent with the purposes of the Lord. 1:1; 15:1-5; 24:1-6.

2. Identity of the blessed:
Jehovah's anointed. 28:8-10; 105:15.

Jacob whom he (Jehovah) loveth. 47:4; 77:15; 105:6; 135:4, 12.

Judah. 76:1.

Zion, the city of God. 48:1-14.

Saints who have made a covenant with Jehovah by sacrifice. 50:5, 14-15; 53:6.

Those who are good and upright in heart. 125: 4; 73:1; 128:1-6.

3. Destiny of the blessed:
To be delivered from enemies by God. 71:1-24.

To be chastened and taught by Jehovah. 94:12-14.

To be preserved in the everlasting kingdom of Jehovah. 145:13, 20.

XLV

Nature, Identity, and Destiny of the Wicked
Nature of the wicked:

One whose pride makes him deny God. 10:4, 11;
14:1-7; 53:1-6; 36:1-4.

One whose mouth is full of cursing, deceit, and
depression. 10:7.

One who murders the innocent. 10:8.

One who seeks to devour the poor. 10:9.

One who deceives by flattery. 12:2.

Those who are of the world, whose portion is in
this life. 17:14.

Those who speak peace while seeking mischief.
28:3.

Those who return evil for good. 35:11-16.

Those that trust in their wealth. 49:6-14.

One who loves wickedness and violence. 58:1-5;
109:16-18; 139:19.

One who worships idols. 97:7; 115:4, 8.

2. Identity of the wicked:
The nations. 2:1-3; 9:5, 17, 19.
Enemies of Israel. 44:5.
Enemies of God. 50:16-21; 68:1.
Those that hate Zion. 129:5.

3. Destiny of the wicked:
To be hated by JHWH. 11:5.
To receive judgment from JHWH. 125:4-5;
10:5.
To return to his earth. 146:4.
To be destroyed by JHWH. 145:20.
To be destroyed by his own evil. 34:21.
To have snares, fire, brimstone, and burning wind
brought upon them by JHWH. 11:6.
To be cast into the pit. 94:13.

. . . .

The Blessing of Messiah's Control Over the Nations

OUTLINE OF PSALM 2

Theme: Messiah and the Nations

1. The nations set themselves unreasonably against the anointed 2:1-3
2. JHWH installs the anointed in Zion despite the nations 2:4-6
3. JHWH promises the nations to the anointed as an inheritance 2:7-9
4. The nations are urged to make peace with the anointed 2:10-12

(Cf. Psalm 9, 10, 33, 46, 65, 66, 78, 87, 100)

THEOLOGICAL STUDIES
XLVI

The Implications of Messianic Control of the Nations

The obvious theme of Psalm 2 is JHWH's use of "his anointed"[1] to control rebellious nations. However, deeper implications are his control of Israel's human king by that same means and likewise his control of all his children.

Control of rebellious nations is so described as to indicate several teachings that are greatly emphasized in Psalms, as follows:

1. The nations are identified with the wicked, because of their rebellion against Jehovah.[2] This does

---

[1]Psalm 2:2.
[2]Psalm 2:1-3.

not condemn the nations of all ages, but was a characterization of those existing at the time of writing; nor does it utterly condemn all the people in the nations, because exceptions are made later. This does condemn rebellion against the true God and his appointed representative in the earth, the anointed one. Such rebellion is condemned by the word "why"[3] as unreasonable folly. "Why" means "for what reason" or "to what end," and it carries with it an implication of reproach, of blame for lack of reason and worthy purpose.

2. The wrath of JHWH will be poured out upon these rebellious nations through the anointed one.[4] This teaches that God will use him to control history and determine the destiny of nations.

3. The nations will become an inheritance of the anointed one.[5] Inheritance means a thing received as one's own. In the Bible it is applied to inheritance of property or to inheritance in the sense of possession of a person or a people. Exodus 34:9 applies it to JHWH's possession of Israel. In this case possession of the nations themselves appears to be the meaning, because their leaders are exhorted immediately afterward to submit and be blessed as others who trust God.

4. It is expected that converted remnants of the nations will be blessed by the anointed one.[6] To "kiss the Son"[7] will acknowledge fealty to this

[3]Psalm 2:1.
[4]Psalm 2:4-6.
[5]Psalm 2:7-9.
[6]Psalm 2:10-12.
[7]Psalm 2:12a.

ordained ruler of earth. Thus men out of the nations will be converted to his rule. Then they will be blessed as all those that "take refuge in him."[8]

This punishment, inheritance, and blessing of the nations obviously requires for its complete fulfilment an anointed one greater than David. David's sin made it clear that someone must save him before his line could become a blessing to the nations. Accordingly, the use of "my Son"[9] and "the Son"[10] to describe the anointed one of this psalm may have been intended to call attention to the expectation of the author that this anointed one would bear a peculiarly close relation to JHWH—a relation that David or any other merely human king could never bear. New Testament authors saw this significance in "my Son" and applied it to Jesus.[11]

The aid of this anointed one greater than David becomes a very important theme in Psalms. It is seemingly illusive at first, but definite when carefully studied. In Psalm 18 it becomes control of enemies. In Psalm 22 it becomes control of the fear of death. In Psalm 23 it becomes control of the king himself; and this theme is richly developed later. In Psalm 29 it is the strength of JHWH imparted through worship; in 32 forgiveness; in 51 an answer to the prayers of the forgiven; in 67 the urge to share salvation with others; in 72 the guarantee of succession; in 73 the cure of doubt; in 103 the inspiration of praise; and in 110 the liberty that

---

[8]Psalm 2:12c.
[9]Psalm 2:7.
[10]Psalm 2:12.
[11]Acts 13:33; Heb. 1:5; 5:5.

is in Christ. Thus Messiah is JHWH's means of fulfilling all his promises to his children.

The example of David has an application to every child of God. Even as messianic control was necessary throughout his days in the flesh to save him from his own sin and to fit him as a means of extending Messiah's blessings unto others, so is messianic control essential to the fulfilment of JHWH's promises concerning every believer.

. . . .

The Blessing of Messiah's Control Over Enemies

OUTLINE OF PSALM 18

Theme: Victory Over Enemies

1. Result of prayer unto JHWH...........18:1-6
2. Result of providential control of the situation 18:7-15
3. Means of protecting JHWH's servant...18:16-19
4. Reward of JHWH's servant for his righteousness 18:20-24
5. Recompense to the ungodly of his own crookedness 18:25-36
6. Means of extending the rule of JHWH's servant 18:37-45
7. Occasion for praising JHWH among the nations 18:46-50
   (Cf. Psalm 5, 17, 27, 34, 35, 56, 57, 68, 69, 94, 109, 129, 139)

THEOLOGICAL STUDIES

XLVII

Vengeance in Psalms

Psalm 18:50 connects David's victory over enemies with JHWH's deliverance and blessing of David's line, even "for evermore." Again as in Psalm 2 the promises to David require the Messiah for their complete fulfilment. We realize, therefore, that when David said, "The angel of Jehovah encampeth round about them that fear him, and delivereth them,"[12] he knew that Messiah was JHWH's means of giving him victory.

These facts show that divine vengeance is the work of Messiah, and they made Psalm 18 to be the center of Old Testament teaching concerning this subject. Along with other passages in Psalms and Romans 12:17 to 13:7, this psalm gives a rounded view of this terrible phase of God's dealing with men.

It is extremely necessary in studying vengeance to look at all sides of the matter. Psalm 18 does this more than any other passage. Here the experiences of David are unified, and the following views are put together in one picture:

1. Responsibility for vengeance is borne by the head of the state. The superscription of Psalm 18 refers to David as "the servant of Jehovah." The use of this term in Samuel shows that it marked David as both anointed to be king and approved in

---

[12]Psalm 34:7.

his work as king. Thus he was in the position of
the one described by Romans 13:4, saying, "He
beareth not the sword in vain, for he is a minister
of God, an avenger for wrath to him that doeth
evil." All the expressions in this psalm and seemingly all similar expressions in Psalms arise from
this viewpoint.

Otherwise, many expressions of the imprecatory
psalms would violate the spirit of the Sixth Commandment, "Thou shalt not kill." We need to remember that this was a command to individuals,
forbidding that any individual take the law into his
own hands. It was a deduction from the statement,
"Vengeance belongeth unto me, I will recompense,
saith the Lord."[13] It did not forbid judicial action
in JHWH's name.

2. Responsibility for vengeance is approached in
the spirit of prayer. Psalm 18 begins with a prayer
for vengeance and concludes with thanksgiving for
its answer. This recognizes the teaching that vengeance belongs to God and that his human instruments must needs have his guidance.

3. Execution of vengeance is seen as a matter
providentially controlled. The storm of Psalm 18:
7-15 is an illustration of the tempests in human
affairs which JHWH overrules so as to assure the
fulfilment of his will. Thus JHWH takes the
enemies of his servant to be his enemies.[14]

---

[13]Heb. 10:30; Rom. 12:19.
[14]Psalm 18:14.

4. Vengeance is seen as necessary to protect JHWH's servant.[15] The government of the servant could not stand without it.

5. This vengeance is described as God's reward of the righteousness of his servant;[16] therefore, it is the execution of God's will by a human agent, rather than wanton or self-willed seeking of revenge.

6. This vengeance is JHWH's way of causing crooks to fall by their own crookedness. Psalm 18: 25-26 teaches this in a very striking way. Perhaps the following translation can make this teaching clearer:

> With a godly man you show yourself favorable;
> With a man of integrity, you reveal your own integrity;
> With a pure man, you show yourself pure;
> But with a crook, you deal tortuously (as a wrestler who twists himself to oppose every movement of his opponent).

This means that God so accommodates himself to the attitudes of men toward him as to fulfil the desires for goodness in the godly and destroy the deceitful aims of the ungodly.

7. This vengeance promotes the spread of the kingdom as well as destroys its enemies.[17]

8. This vengeance is a fitting part of the gospel message to the nations.[18]

[15]Psalm 18:16-19.
[16]Psalm 18:20-24.
[17]Psalm 18:43-45.
[18]Psalm 18:49.

With these thoughts from Psalm 18 should be put many teachings from other psalms. A few outstanding ones are as follows:

1. All descriptions of the nature and identity of the wicked indicate that the enemies of the king are identified in his thinking with the wicked. Thus the enemies of the king are the enemies of God. Psalm 68 makes these thoughts very pointed.

2. The hope that victory over enemies would result in the submission and salvation of many is brought out very forcefully in Psalm 2:7-12. Verses 10-12 show that it is the earnest desire of the psalmist, at the same moment that he predicts the destruction of the nations, that every person who will shall be brought into the kingdom of the anointed. It is evident that only the incorrigible are expected to suffer the vengeance of God.

3. The fact that families of the enemies of God are sometimes spoken of as if they too are the enemies of God is the most difficult point in the whole matter. Psalm 69; 109 are outstanding in their expression of this thought. They seem to many to express a feeling which cannot be reconciled with Christian views of individual responsibility for sin and the obligation of all of the forgiven to forgive others. The problem is admittedly difficult. However, remembering that the experiences of David are the ones that give unity to all these points, interpreters may rightfully stress the following as matters which must be balanced with his attitude concerning these families of the wicked:

(1) Even while saying,

Let their habitation be desolate;
Let none dwell in their tents; (Psalm 69:25)

the psalmist adds,

The meek have seen it and are glad; ye that
seek after God, let your heart live;

For Jehovah heareth the needy, and despiseth
not his prisoners. (Psalm 69:32-33)

Thus Psalm 69 as a whole seems to leave opportunity for the sparing and saving of any Rahab who would come out from among the heathen and accept the God of Israel.

(2) David's actions likewise exemplified mercy and forgiveness where it appeared that such would not undermine his kingdom and overthrow his rule. His putting Shemei on probation is an example. (Cf. 2 Sam. 19:16-23.) In this case an enemy, unchanged in heart but begging for mercy, is granted all the mercy his actions will permit.

(3) The cutting off of children and widows, as expressed in Psalm 109:9-15, is a result of views concerning the solidarity of the family which had come down from ancient times.

Behind this view of the solidarity of the family lay the experiences of the children of God with heathen peoples, whereby they knew that as a rule all members of ungodly families in Israel or out of it were so affected by the influences of heathendom that they would continue in its ways. These experiences led to the conviction that the people of God were morally obligated to wage holy war against

those peoples who had proved themselves to be
morally reprobate. (Cf. Ex. 17:8-16, Deut. 25:17-
19, Num. 31:1-54.) Likewise they led, as in the
case of Achan in Joshua 7:16-26, to the execution
of whole families for crimes committed by the head
of the family.

These convictions are evidence that those holding them were convinced that the elimination of the
reprobates in their midst was necessary to prevent
contamination of the children of God.

Unquestionably the magnanimity of Christian
mercies favors mercy in all cases where no uncon-
trollable threat to other lives is thought to exist.
Nevertheless, this ideal of Christian mercy admits
the possible existence of conditions under which its
application would be unwise, because the children of
God would be endangered. Thus the same principle
rules over exceptions now as in David's day. The
fact that such conditions were more prevalent then
does not change the principle.

. . . .

The Blessing of Messiah's Control Over Death

OUTLINE OF PSALM 22

Theme: Triumph Over Death

I

Over Fear of Being Forsaken by God in Time of
Death

1. His prayers are unanswered............22:1-2
2. His trust is mocked...................22:3-8
   (1) He confesses faith in God.........22:3

(2) He believes God saved the
fathers 22:4-5
(3) Yet he is left as a worm among
men 22:6-8
Con. Still, he clings to faith inspired
in him from birth............22:9-11

II

Over Fear as to What Men Can Do to the Body in
Time of Death

1. He is surrounded by bulls of Bashan.......22:12
2. He is about to be swallowed as by lions..22:13
3. He is scared to death...................22:14
4. He is utterly exhausted.................22:15
5. He is stretched and chewed as by dogs.....22:16
6. He is stripped and gazed at as a body
committed to death....................22:17
7. His garments are disposed of as no longer needed 22:18
Con. Nevertheless, he prophesies deliverance 22:19-21

III

Over Fear to Tell the Story of One's Convictions
About Death

1. He promises to preach to his brethren..22:22-26
2. He predicts the spread of the kingdom..22:27-31
(1) To the ends of the earth.........22:27
(2) Among the nations (Gentiles)....22:28
(3) To the living and the dying.....22:29

(4) To the promised seed............22:30
Con. He foresees the evangelization
    of unborn generations...........22:31
(Cf. Psalm 16, 17, 42, 43, 44, 113-118.)

THEOLOGICAL STUDIES

XLVIII

Victory Over the Fear of Death

The great victory of Psalm 22 is victory over the fear of death rather than death itself. The danger of the fear of death arose out of David's mortal struggles with enemies, and it threatened to make him doubt God's continued care for him, to make him fear man, and to cause failure to proclaim his faith to others. Step by step Psalm 22 records his victory over these temptations.

To understand Psalm 22 it is necessary to study it from David's viewpoint, seeing each detail as a reflection of a danger he faced. For instance, "pierced" my hands and my feet[19] was not written as a description of the driving of spikes through Jesus' hands and feet. The word for "pierced" describes the piercing of dogs' teeth through a victim they have caught. These dogs are David's enemies. One time he calls them bulls,[20] this time dogs, another time men,[21] another time lions,[22] another time unicorns;[23] but always they are enemies.

---

[19]Psalm 22:16.
[20]Psalm 22:12.
[21]Psalm 22:18.
[22]Psalm 22:21a.
[23]Psalm 22:21b.

At the same time it is Jesus' conquest of death itself that fulfils the faith by which David conquered the fear of death. After quoting Psalm 22:1 as a description of his experience of being forsaken by God, for a time, Jesus went beyond the experiences of David, even unto death and resurrection. Thus suffering as one "made to be sin on our behalf that we might become the righteousness of God in him,"[24] he fulfilled David's faith that God would not forsake him in death; he demonstrated the futility of the worst men can do the body; and he provided the triumphant cry of those who would evangelize, saying, "Death is swallowed up in victory. O death, where is thy victory? O death, where is thy sting? . . . Thanks be to God who giveth us the victory through our Lord Jesus Christ."[25]

[24] 2 Cor. 5:21.
[25] 1 Cor. 15:54-57.

.   .   .   .

The Blessing of Messiah's Control Over the King

OUTLINE OF PSALM 23

Theme: The Good Shepherd

1. Gives everything one needs..............23:1
2. Gives food and rest.....................23:2
3. Gives refreshing and guidance............23:3
4. Gives confidence and strength............23:4
5. Gives security and abundance............23:5
6. Gives lifelong and everlasting companionship 23:6
   (Cf. Psalm 3, 4, 25, 30, 31, 46, 80, 85, 90, 119, 139.)

THEOLOGICAL STUDIES

XLIX

Comfort of the Shepherd's Rod and Staff

Beginning with Psalm 23, Messiah's control over the sins of the king looms up as a far greater matter than his control of the king's enemies or anything his enemies may do to him. The background of this matter is in the complex conditions described by 2 Samuel, 10-24. The analysis of it is in great psalms like 29, 32, 51, 67, 73, 103. There is a simple but inexpressibly profound illustration of it in these words of Psalm 23:4, "Thy rod and thy staff, they comfort me."

Jesus' use of the figure of the good shepherd in the tenth chapter of John's Gospel to describe his care for his sheep reveals the messianic application of this psalm.

The comfort of the rod and staff is first of all a turning of the sheep from sin. The rod was a short heavy club fitted for punishment. The rod stands for a chastening influence. The use of the rod is seen in the proverb, "Spare the rod and spoil the child."[26] Micah prays, saying, "Feed [Rule or Shepherd] thy people with thy rod,"[27] while thinking of JHWH's chastening of his people by captivity and exile. Psalm 32:1-4 fits here.

This comfort is also a strengthening of the nature of the sheep. The staff stands for a sustaining and strengthening influence. As the shepherd leaned

[26]Prov.
[27]Micah 7:14.

upon his staff and was strengthened by it, so his sheep lean upon his help and are strengthened by it. Thus, as in Psalm 29, the children of God by worship lay hold upon the strength of God.

This comfort is thus an influence that allays every fear. The sheep says, "Yea, though I walk through the valley of the shadow of death, I will fear no evil; for thou art with me."[28] Psalm 73:23-26 gives a wonderful expression of the assurance it imparts. Jesus gives it its most perfect expression, saying, "I give unto them eternal life; and they shall never perish, and no one shall snatch them out of my hand."[29]

.   .   .   .

The Blessing of Worship
OUTLINE OF PSALM 29

Theme: Meaning of Worship

1. Recognition of the source of spiritual blessings 29:1-2
   (1) In JHWH himself..............29:1
   (2) In the worship of JHWH........29:2

2. Vision of the exercise of JHWH's power in
   the storms of life......................29:3-9

3. Appropriation of the strength of JHWH.29:10-11
   (1) Of his everlasting rule 29:10
   (2) Of his peace.................29:11

(Cf. Psalm 15, 19, 24, 48, 50, 61, 77, 84, 91.)

[28]Psalm 23:4a.
[29]John 10:28.

THEOLOGICAL STUDIES

L

The Peace of JHWH Worshipers

Psalm 29 pictures the peace of the children of God as arising out of their worship of JHWH.

The source of spiritual strength is described as being not merely in JHWH himself[30] but in worship of him. [31] In other words, the strength of God cannot operate in man till he opens the way by worship.

The storm of 29:3-9 is obviously intended as an illustration of the teaching of the psalm, and it fits as an illustration of man's vision of the power of JHWH overruling his own tempestuous experiences so as to lead to his acknowledgment of that overruling as a revelation of JHWH's glory. In doing so man realizes that God still controls his world and makes it fulfil his purpose for man.

Acceptance of this rule of JHWH over himself and the world as everlasting is then said to give man peace.[32] Worship puts JHWH on the throne of man's life as well as the throne of the universe, and naturally his heart is made to be at ease in any storm that may arise.

---

[30]Psalm 29:1.
[31]Psalm 29:2.
[32]Psalm 29:10-11.

. . . .

The Blessing of Forgiveness
OUTLINE OF PSALM 32
Theme: JHWH's Cure for Sin

1. Chastening pressure on the silent sinner...32:1-4
2. Immediate forgiveness of the repentant confessor 32:5
3. Protective care of the prayerful heart....32:6-7
4. Intimate guidance of the yielded will....32:8-11
   (Cf. Psalm 3, 4, 8, 38, 51, 103.)

THEOLOGICAL STUDIES
LI

Forgiveness is JHWH's Assurance of Preservation

Psalm 32 gives one of the finest descriptions of JHWH's ways of preserving his children from sin. It shows us how fitting it would be for us to speak of the preservation of the saints rather than the perseverance of the saints, because it stresses the fact that this blessed assurance depends upon the Lord rather than upon us.

Feature points in this picture are as follows:

1. The pressure of JHWH's hand on the sinning child who tries to avoid confession.[33]   32:4a would be better translated this way, "For day and night thy hand continued to be heavy upon me." This portrays JHWH as making the pressure of chastisement heavier and heavier until he gets results.

2. The granting of forgiveness at the moment of confession. The "forgavest" of 32:5 is a perfect in-

-----
[33]Psalm 32:3-4.

dicating this immediate forgiveness. It indicates that the only condition of forgiveness that can be lacking in a child of God is acknowledgment of his sin.

3. The child of God who fails to seek forgiveness as soon as he is aware of having sinned brings trouble on himself. The clause, "in a time when thou mayest be found,"[34] is literally "at the time of finding," and it appears in this context to refer to the discovery of sin. The godly are implored to pray for forgiveness the moment they know they have sinned, being assured of protection by their loving Saviour.

4. The counsel of the forgiven by JHWH produces guidance which JHWH says is given "with mine eye."[35] Understanding between two persons must be intimate and mutual for one to guide the other with the eye.

.   .   .   .

The Blessing of Prayer

OUTLINE OF PSALM 51

Theme: The Prayers of a Repentant Child of God

1. Prayer for mercy 51:1
2. Prayer for cleansing 51:2-4
   (1) Thorough cleansing..............51:2
   (2) Cleansing of the conscience......51:3
   (3) Cleansing of the attitude toward God 51:4
3. Prayer for purity.....................51:5-7

---

[34]Psalm 32:6.
[35]Psalm 32:8.

   (1) Purification from the depravity
      of human nature 51:5
   (2) Purity in secret places..........51:6
   (3) Perfect purity 51:7
4. Prayer for joy 51:8-12
   (1) Joy after chastening............51:8
   (2) Joy over atonement for sin.......51:9
   (3) Joy of a new creature..........51:10
   (4) Joy of God's presence and Spirit.51:11
   (5) Joy of a willing spirit..........51:12
5. Prayer for power to testify...........51:13-17
   (1) So that sinners will be converted.51:13
   (2) So as to sing of God's
      righteousness 51:14
   (3) So as to praise God's delight in a
      broken and contrite heart.....51:15-17
6. Prayer for Zion.....................51:18-19
   (Cf. Psalm 38, 39, 40, 41, 65, 86, 103, 143,
   145.)

THEOLOGICAL STUDIES
LII
Forgiveness is Assurance of an Answer to Every Prayer

Pslam 51 expresses the attitude of the child of God that has been brought back by chastisement to desire for fellowship with the Lord.

This attitude is one of prayer. Having tasted the bitter results of self-directed efforts to hide and forget sin, the repentant one begs the Lord to "blot out"[36] his sins. This blotting out may be understood

---
[36]Psalm 51:1.

as meaning first of all the covering provided by
JHWH's forgiveness, which assures him it is not
held against him. However, the child of God is led
afterward to understand that this blotting out gives
assurance of much more, even the complete removal
of sin eventually. One psalm after another shows
the ever-widening and deepening of this assurance.

This prayer is an appeal for mercy according to
the lovingkindness (grace) of JHWH,[37] according
to the multitude of his tender mercies.[38] It recognizes that there is no other basis for forgiveness. That
is why its granting is so certain, once God's child
has asked for it. That is why its assurance is so
rich in meaning. That is why God's child may fittingly couch his prayer in the words of an imperative. Once the repentant sinner has realized the
yearning of JHWH to forgive, the willingness of
JHWH always to forgive a trusting one, he knows
JHWH is happy to be commanded in accord with
his will to save sinners.

This prayer grows and grows in its requests as
the supplicant realizes that JHWH's grant of forgiveness is truly an answer to every prayer an obedient child of God can ask. It becomes a prayer for
cleansing,[39] for purity,[40] for joy,[41] for power to testify,[42] for Zion or the whole congregation of God's
redeemed.[43] In other psalms it becomes a prayer for

[37]Psalm 51:1a.
[38]Psalm 51:1b.
[39]Psalm 51:2-4.
[40]Psalm 51:5-7.
[41]Psalm 51:8-12.
[42]Psalm 51:13-17.
[43]Psalm 51:18-19.

JHWH's blessing on all peoples,[44] for godly successors on the throne of the kingdom,[45] for assurance of JHWH's control of eternal destiny.[46] Finally it becomes a thanksgiving for assurance of JHWH's perfection of all who are his.[47]   Everywhere this prayer breathes conviction that the things it asks for are assured the moment they are requested.

Surely we may add that the Lord's problem is not the granting of what a believing child asks for, but to induce his child to ask and to believe.

. . . .

The Blessing of Missions
OUTLINE OF PSALM 67

Theme: A Prayer for Worldwide Missions

I. A plea that God be gracious to us........67:1
II. A purpose that others be saved through
   us 67:2-4
III. A prophesy that thus shall the earth
   produce her God-appointed fruitage....67:5-7
   (Cf. Psalm 18:43-50; 22:22-31; 25:8-14;
   35:27, 28; 47:1-9; 66:1-20; 100:1-5; 145:
   9-21)

THEOLOGICAL STUDIES
LIII

Forgiveness is a Compelling Reason for Sharing Salvation

The high significance of Psalm 67 is in the relations of man's will to God's aid in the missionary en-

---

[44]Psalm 67.
[45]Psalm 72.
[46]Psalm 73.
[47]Psalm 103.

terprise. The movements of man's will are related here to God's answers to his prayers as the movements of a fine watch are related to its jewels. They pivot, turn, and depend for all their efficacy upon those jewels of God's aid.

There are three great movements of man's will involved: a plea, a purpose, and a prophecy. These appear as follows:

1. A plea that God will bless the people who are already his. The prayer of 67:1 is not a mere petition, but is framed in words of urgency that seek to persuade God to fulfil the desire of the one interceding.

2. An urging of God to let his purpose to use his own people to evangelize others be fulfilled by the reproduction of it in their own wills. 67:2 states that such use of God's own people is God's purpose in blessing them. When it says, "that," it means "in order that" and indicates this purpose.

3. Acceptance by faith of God's decree that the kingdom of God shall be established on earth. Another urging of God in 67:5 to let the peoples of the earth be evangelized through his own redeemed ones leads to a declaration of faith in 67:6-7 that this shall be accomplished. When the psalmist says, "The earth hath yielded her increase," he uses a prophetic perfect which says that God has decreed this fulfilment. In other words, he sees the acceptance of missionary responsibility by God's people as leading by God's help to the winning of the world for God.

Before, between, and after these movements of man's will there are great enabling acts of God: forgiveness, grace, control of the nations, and establishment of the kingdom. These appear as follows:

1. Forgiveness, as shown in Psalm 51, is the influence that moves the child of God to prayer for others.

2. Grace continued or the extension of forgiveness is taken for granted as the answer to the prayer of 67:1. This grace is seen as the power that moves God's people unto fulfilment of the purpose seen in 67:2, "that thy way may be known upon the earth, thy salvation among all nations." God's forgiving grace becomes the jewel upon which his children's sense of missionary responsibility rests and moves. This accords with the teaching of Jesus, when he said, "As thou [God the Father] didst send me into the world, even so send I them into the world."[48]

3. Control or rule of the nations, which the intercessor saw as resulting from the purpose to evangelize the nations. This is described in 67:4.

4. Establishment of the kingdom on earth. This is prophesied in 67:6 and described in 67:7 as extending to the ends of the earth.

Conclusion

These enabling acts of God are indeed set like the jewels of the watch. They hold in place the movements of redeemed wills as a diamond does the spindle of a watch's wheel. Moreover, their purpose is more adamant than any diamond. At the same

---

[48]John 17:18.

time they permit a freedom of movement to a redeemed will like the ease of movement a diamond
allows the pivot of that spindle. Yea, their adjustment to the regenerated human will is more perfect
than the adjustment of any jewel to its pivot.

.   .   .   .

The Blessing of Succession

OUTLINE OF PSALM 72

Theme: Prayer for Blessings of Godly Rule

1. For righteous judgments 72:1-4
2. For everlasting fear 72:5-7
3. For universal dominion 72:8-11
4. For benevolent care 72:12-14
5. For abundant fruitfulness 72:15-16
6. For perpetual succession 72:17
7. For divine overruling 72:18-19
   (Cf. Psalm 20, 21, 45, 89.)

THEOLOGICAL STUDIES

LIV

Divine Provision for a Succession of Rulers

"Psalm 72 sees the blessings of David, the "sure
mercies of David"[49] as Isaiah calls them, assured to
his line forever. Psalm 89:19-37 expands this idea
at length. It is far from being what is sometimes
called the divine right of kings, but it does signify
a divine provision for those rulers who help to establish the kingdom of God on earth.

---

[49]Isa. 5.

The source of this provision is indicated by the fact that this psalm is a prayer throughout. In verse 1 the attitude of prayer is obvious. As the note of ASV on the "he will" of verse 2 indicates, all similar expressions in this psalm may be framed in the words of prayer. Those in 72:8, 15-17 must be so to be true to the original. Thus is this psalm characterized by appeals to God to provide the blessings whereby his rulers shall rule.

The objects of this provision are the true successors of David. 72:1 names both "the king" and "the king's son" without calling individual names. It points thus to all those in the succession.

The certainty of this provision is expressed by the same prayers mentioned above. Most of them may be translated either as petitions or as affirmations. As affirmations they express the certainty the author feels about God's granting the blessings requested. Expectation of their granting pervades his prayer.

The perfections of this provision are marvelous. We need mention only its righteousness, universality, and permanence to see that it involves an ideal state that can be fully realized only in the kingdom of God.

The means of this provision must be the messianic control implied by Psalm 2. Thus it is that we are made to know that all the blessings foreseen in Psalms—those for individuals, for Israel, for the nations, and for succeeding generations—are to be

made available by the ideal, the perfect, the divine
Ruler of rulers, the King of kings.

.   .   .   .

The Blessing of Assurance
OUTLINE OF PSALM 73
Theme: An Experience with Doubt
Introduction
"God is good to Israel"....................73:1
I
Upset by Pessimism
Int. Confession by the psalmist of back-
sliding, being almost an apostate..........73:2
1. Envious of evil men 73:3-12
  (1) Of their completeness............73:3
  (2) Of their physical strength........73:4
  (3) Of their freedom from trouble....73:5
  (4) Of their pride...................73:6
  (5) Of their abundance 73:7
  (6) Of their power 73:8
  (7) Of their "big talk" 73:9
  (8) Of their influence 73:10
  (9) Of their boldness 73:11
  (10) Of their success 73:12
2. Doubtful about the value of his own
  goodness 73:13-14
  (1) Of his sincerity and innocence...73:13
  (2) Of his willingness to be chastened.73:14
II
Uplifted by Prayer
1. Rejection of his former thought as
  treachery 73:15

2. Determination to think the problem
   through 73:16
3. Prayer for a vision of the end of evil men..73:17
4. Vision of the final destruction of wickedness 73:18-20
   (1) As providentially prepared 73:18
   (2) As utterly consuming 73:19
   (3) As revealing God's contempt 73:20

III
Upheld by Providence

Int. Condemnation of his pessimism as foolish,
   ignorant, and brutish 73:21-22
1. Vision of himself as continually upheld
   by God 73:23
2. Vision of himself as guided all the way to
   glory 73:24
3. Vision of God as satisfying all desire......73:25
4. Vision of God as the strength of his
   heart forever 73:26

Conclusion

Announcement of trust and purpose to
   testify 73:27-28
   (Cf. Psalm 36, 37.)

THEOLOGICAL STUDIES
LV
Antidotes for Pessimism

All the psalms previously studied have contributed to the assurance that JHWH will bring about,
despite all opposition, the fulfilment of the blessings

he promises to believers. Psalm 73 deals with one of the most paralyzing oppositions to his work of grace that ever arises. This is doubt—doubt in the heart of his own child. Of course his work cannot go forward in that heart till doubt is conquered. However, his preparations for uprooting it and casting it out forever may go forward even while doubt is there; and this is one of the great lessons of Psalm 73.

In 73:1 the author exclaims, saying, "Surely God is good to Israel," as though he would that the reader hold fast to that central thought while he proceeds to confess the doubt that once afflicted him.

As though to guard against other possible misunderstandings he adds a statement that Israel is the "pure in heart"—the spiritual Israel, not those who are Israelites merely because of physical descent. These are they to whom God is so good.

Then he illustrates in 73:2 his experience with doubt by saying, "My steps had well nigh slipped." Literally this is, "My steps had been poured out as nothing." It means that he had been as when a fellow slips on ice and suddenly finds his feet where his head ought to be, and he is trying to walk on nothing. Even so had the pessimism recited in 73: 3-14 upset him. The cause is given in 73:3 as envy of the wicked, and this envy of the prosperity of evil men had upset him seriously.

In 73:15 he makes a sudden turn of thought. He indicates that, if he had actually and finally accepted the pessimism that passed through his mind, he would have been a traitor to the generation of God's children, a Benedict Arnold among those truly born of God. Then he tells us what brought about this great turn, this cure of his doubt—providence and prayer. Prayer is mentioned first, but it brings a vision of a providence that reveals him to be continually with God or accompanied by God; a providence that held his hand even when he doubted; yea, a providence that will guide him all the way to glory. Prayer opens his eyes to all this and relieves every fear.

These conclusions accord with 1 John 3:20, "If our heart condemn us, God is greater than our heart, and knoweth all things." Likewise, they are an illustration of Jesus' word in John 10:28, saying of his sheep, "No one shall snatch them out of my hand."

.   .   .   .

The Blessing of Praise
OUTLINE OF PSALM 103

Theme: Inspirations for Blessing JHWH

Int. A call to one's own soul to bless JHWH's
    holy name 103:1-2
1. JHWH's forgiveness....................103:3
2. JHWH's redemption 103:4
3. JHWH's renewal of life 103:5
4. JHWH's righteous protection 103:6
5. JHWH's abundant mercies 103:7-10
   (1) Revealed to Israel 103:7, 8
   (2) Tempering his anger 103:9
   (3) Not according to our sins 103:10

6. JHWH's immeasurable grace.........103:11-14
   (1) Higher than the heavens 103:11
   (2) As far as the east is from the west 103:12
   (3) Like as a father pitieth his
      children 103:13-14
7. JHWH's everlasting lovingkindness...103:15-18
   (1) To perishing men 103:15-16
   (2) To those who fear him 103:17
   (3) To those who keep his covenant.103:18
Con. A call to all creation to bless JHWH's
   rule over heaven and earth 103:19-22
   (1) To angels of JHWH 103:19-20
   (2) To all the hosts of JHWH......103:21
   (3) To all the works of JHWH......103:22
(Cf. Psalm 33, 95-100, 104-107, 119-136, 145-150.)

THEOLOGICAL STUDIES

LVI

How Does Man Bless God?

The call in Psalm 103:1-2, 22 to the psalmist's own soul to bless JHWH gives occasion for an interesting and profitable question, How does a man bless God? Out of the psalm several answers arise, as follows:

1. By accepting the grace of God.

To bless means to pronounce holy. The author of Psalm 103 praises God because he has accepted the grace of God and learned how wonderful his grace is. That acceptance reflects belief that the giver of it is holy and is the source of all holiness.

2. By showing gratitude for the grace of God.

To bless means to make happy. The praise of Psalm 103 is an effort to express the gratitude of the psalmist for the grace he has received and to bring happiness thereby to the giver. How much such gratitude means to God is expressed in a superlatively beautiful way when he is called in Psalm 22:3 "the one that inhabitest the praises of Israel."

3. By glorifying the grace of God.

To bless means to glorify. When Psalm 103: 11-14 extols the grace of God by saying that it is higher than the heavens, as far as the east is from the west, and like as a father pitieth his children, it truly gives a picture in keeping with the immeasurable glories of the grace itself.

A German professor of higher mathematics is said to have lost his position and even his self-respect through drunkenness. Shame and restlessness drove him away from home and country. In an American city one winter night he wandered through the streets as a tramp. Passing a church, he decided to slip into a back seat where he could be warm for an hour. However, he was converted that night and became a regular attendant upon the services of worship in that church. Later in a prayer meeting the pastor happened to quote Psalm 103:12; and, seeing the former professor, he said, "Professor, how far is the east from the west?" The impulse of former habits made the man grab a pencil and notebook and begin filling out one of the formulas of higher mathematics for measuring great distances. Then

suddenly he stopped and cried: "O pastor, it can't
be done. If you should start from the east and go
toward the west, you might travel the earth around
and come back to your starting point, and all the
while west would be ahead of you. You could not
catch up with it. You could not measure its dis-
tance. And, thank God, that is just how far God
has put away my sins from me!"

The grace of JHWH's forgiveness is just as perfect, just as immeasurable as that. No wonder then
that this psalm is pure praise throughout! There is
not a petition in it. It seems to reflect a realization
that JHWH's grace has already granted more than
heart could wish. It is full to the brim of tributes
of glory.

. . . .

The Blessing of Messiah's Control Over the World
OUTLINE OF PSALM 110
Theme: The Authority of Messiah
1. Ordained by JHWH 110:1
2. To be extended from Jerusalem 110:2
3. To be supported by an army of volunteers.110:3
4. To be the rule of a priest-king 110:4
5. To prevail over all earthly powers........110:5
6. To destroy all enemies 110:6
7. To win after a desperate struggle.........110:7

THEOLOGICAL STUDIES
LVII
Liberty in Christ
Dictionaries, lexicons, law, and literature bring
out three great words in trying to define liberty:

namely, choice, ability, and right. However, their use of these words does not always harmonize. What do these words have to do with one another? Does one have the right to choose to do whatever he has the ability to do? That "might makes right" philosophy makes a Hitler. What is right? This is the question! Does accidental opportunity confer the prerogatives of freedom?

Psalm 110 offers an answer. It is not on the surface of the text but in the implications of its teaching. Put together clearly, these implications suggest a biblical basis for definitions of liberty which unifies the conflicting ideologies that have grown up around the idea of liberty. Each verse has a suggestion. They are as follows:

1. Right based upon divine authority.

When the authority of Jesus to cleanse the Temple was challenged, as recorded in Matthew 21:23, a word was used for authority which is our word for liberty in the full Christian sense. While Jesus at first declined to answer, seeing that his enemies were not willing to answer his question about the baptism of John, he did finally as recorded in Matthew 22:41-46 give to discerning minds an indication of his answer. He used Psalm 110:1 so as to present evidence of his messiahship. In other words, the decree of Jehovah, saying, "Sit thou on my right hand until I make thine enemies the footstool of thy feet," conferred upon Jesus the authority; i.e., the liberty, to rule the world.

The conception of liberty as authority from God is sharply distinguished in Scripture—as students of the Word know full well—from that idea of liberty ascribed by 2 Peter 2:18-19 to false prophets. The distinction is that between the English words "right" and "license," between the Greek words *exousia* and *eleutheria,* and between the Hebrew words *rishyon* and *deror.*

2. Ability to put divinely ordained right into practice.

When verse 2 says, "Jehovah will send forth the rod of thy strength out of Zion," it appears to employ as an illustration the act of a sovereign in sending his scepter by a messenger into a foreign realm that the subjects of that foreign realm may indicate submission of themselves to his rule by doing obeisance to this symbol of his authority. Jesus fulfilled this picture when he said, "All authority hath been given unto me in heaven and on earth. Go ye therefore, and make disciples . . . , baptizing them . . . teaching them. . . . "[50] He delegated to human messengers responsibility for proving the possibilities for extension of his authority (liberty).

Because the Great Commission has been preached almost exclusively to the church, we have fallen into the habit of thinking of it as applying only to the church. Nevertheless, the things Jesus commanded cover our life as citizens as well as our life as church members. Not until Christians interpret citizenship

[50]Matt. 28:18-20.

in the light of Christ's authority can they expect to have clear ideas of civil liberty. Theirs is the obligation for carrying the scepter of Christ into that foreign realm as surely as it is their obligation to carry the gospel to sinners.

3. Choice mutually exercised by sovereign and subjects.

When Psalm 110:3 says, "Thy people offer themselves willingly in the day of thy power," harmony appears between the divine ordination of liberty and the human exercise of it. This harmony appears in democracy.

Divine ordination appears here in the word "power." This word for power means ability and efficiency based upon moral worth. It is that kind of power of personality that elicits the allegiance of followers. It manifests its worth so as to persuade all concerned that its exercise is worthwhile for all. Compulsion, coercion, and dictation have no place in it.

Human exercise appears here in the word "offer themselves willingly." It might well be translated this way, "are free will offerings."[51] It means that Messiah's people are volunteers in the day of his power. By their own free choice he rules over them. This spirit of willing devotion makes his latent authority to reign in power.

This mutual sharing of democracy by sovereign and subject is illustrated here by surpassingly beautiful figures of speech. "In holy array," may be in-

[51]Footnote of ASV.

tended to picture the volunteer followers as clothed in priestly garments. If so, these garments symbolize their responsibility for priestly duties, as follows: (1) interceding with their sovereign on behalf of others; (2) teaching others to subject themselves to their sovereign. These are vital functions in a democracy. Another meaning for this term, "in holy array,"—and the most probable one—is in the beauty of holy character. Thus it describes liberty in Christ as being the adornment of moral integrity. That is the finest fruit of spiritual democracy. The other poetic picture, "Out of the womb of the morning thou hast the dew of thy youth," is a bloom from the same bush. It may describe the freshness, the pervasiveness, the invigorating influence, the sparkling reflective glory of dewdrops in the morning sun, and ascribe these to followers of Christ. It may also say that, instead of being born into this service of the will of man—i.e., by heredity or draft, —they are born into it of the will of God, even as the dew arising so quietly and mysteriously out of the womb of the morning is reckoned by the poet to be accounted for only by the will of God. This is democracy in an ideal setting.

It is vitally important that the dual nature of this liberty be remembered. In this lyric setting we catch visions of the benefits of democracy, all drawn from the consent of the people. We like to emphasize the consent of the people. However, this consent is here linked with something we do not so often emphasize, the rule of the Christ. To lose sight of that would mean the loss of the whole thing eventually.   We must needs remember that the people of this democracy are the Lord's people; these volunteers willingly follow him; these holy characters obtain their holiness from him; these dewdrops out of the womb of the morning are Christians.

4. A priestly function that prevails through love, sacrifice, and persuasion.

When Psalm 110:4 says, "Thou art a priest forever," it signifies the union of regal and priestly functions in Christ.   This presents the functions of state and church as both harmonized and complementary under the rule of Christ.   Also this makes followers of the Christ to be priests of democracy in the state as well as in the church, for Jesus said, "As thou [the Father] has sent me into the world, even so have I also sent them into the world."[52]

Many say that this ideal is eschatological and beyond the reach of today's realistic thinking.   No matter how the fulfilment may be, the preparation is a very present need.   As the Levitical priests were the teachers of old, so the teachers of the Word of God function as the priests of democracy.   As the officiating priests were the ones who brought sacrifices to the altar in Old Testment times, so the preachers of the Word of God who bring men into subjection to the Lordship of Christ are priests of democracy in New Testament times.

5. An executive function destined to prevail over all earthly powers.

[52]John 17:18.

When Psalm 110:5 says, "The Lord will strike through kings in the day of his wrath," it uses a Hebrew prophetic perfect for its verb. In other words, the strongest expression of prophetic faith was used to indicate unquestioning assurance that the authority (liberty) of the Christ would eventually triumph over all earthly powers. Surely a lover of Christian democracy can rest in this promise of God, no matter what troubled seas our ship of state must sail.

6. A judicial function destined to eradicate irreconcilable elements.

When Psalm 110:6 says, "He will judge among the nations, he will fill the places with dead bodies," it describes the eradication of irreconcilable elements as a responsibility of messianic authority (liberty). This may involve capital punishment of reprobate individuals who seek to destroy their fellow beings, or it may involve war against those who would destroy all believers in Christian democracy. This is a solemn and awful responsibility. Nevertheless, it is also a God-imposed obligation upon those deputized by the head of the state to execute sentences imposed by the state under circumstances righteously calculated to indicate the vengeance of God.

7. A source of inner strength that guarantees survival and victory.

When Psalm 110:7 says, "He will drink of the brook in the way: therefore will he lift up the head," it portrays both the life-sapping struggle involved in the effort to establish Christian democracy and

the assurance of ultimate victory. Waters flowing
in the way along which the Son of God goes forth
to war bring a revival of strength. In other words,
the very struggle for establishment of Christian
democracy in others opens hitherto unseen sources
of strength within oneself that guarantee survival
and victory.

THE END

74124
188